LIBRARY

Altruism

CONCEPTS IN THE SOCIAL SCIENCES

Series editor: Frank Parkin

Altruism

Niall Scott and Jonathan Seglow

Open University Press
McGraw-Hill Education
McGraw-Hill House
Shoppenhangers Road
Maidenhead
Berkshire
England
SL6 2QL

email: enquiries@openup.co.uk
world wide web: www.openup.co.uk

and
Two Penn Plaza, New York, NY 10121—2289, USA
First published 2007

A catalogue record of this book is available from the British Library

ISBN–13: 978 0 335 22249 0 (pb) 978 0 335 22250 6 (hb)
ISBN–10: 0335 222498 (pb) 0335 222501 (hb)

Typeset by Kerrypress, Luton, Bedfordshire
Printed in Poland by OZGraf S.A.
www.polskabook.pl

Contents

ALTRUISM

Niall Scott and Jonathan Seglow

Altruism: a brief history

Almost everyone wants to be an altruist, and most of us lament the fact that we are not more altruistic than we are. Non-altruists feel an urge to justify their behaviour to the rest of us, and perhaps they show a little altruism in doing even that. The number of people in the world who unashamedly celebrate their egoistic behaviour is rather small. In this short book we investigate what this thing *is* that so many of us want to be. Is altruism the morally best thing? Not always, as we shall see.

Altruism is a simple idea. Many concepts in philosophy and the social sciences, by contrast, are quite complex. In some cases they arose only with specific forms of social and economic organization and can only be understood in these contexts (think of socialism or citizenship or the state). With others, their adherents argue vehemently over the best conceptions of the basic concept and competing theories are constructed under common names: democracy, social justice, or multiculturalism, for example. Other concepts are not complex but are subject to denials, on the part of their enemies, that there is any value or utility in them at all: postmodernism, welfare, or nationalism, for example. Altruism is not like these cases. It is valued by (almost) everyone and its core meaning universally agreed. Altruism, in its broadest sense, means promoting the interests of the other. That, at least, was what was first meant by the idea. The French term *'altruisme'* was coined by Auguste Comte in his *Système de Politique Positive* ([1851] 1969–70): it combined the Latin *alter* with *ui* and literally meant 'to this other'. The English 'altruism' was first introduced into Britain by George H. Lewes, a popularizer of Comte's work, in 1853 (Brosnahan 1907). Altruism, as Comte intended it (see below), is therefore a moral concept, indeed this may seem to be its central usage.

However, while altruism is an elemental moral idea, it is, nonetheless, embroiled in some thorny questions of right and wrong. Consider the racist organ donor, for example, who wishes to donate their organs, but only to those of their own race, regardless of the need others may have. They are altruistic, but hardly moral. Moreover, while it is easy to condemn this person's racism, consider the huge sums charitably donated by US citizens to beneficiaries in their own society who are, by global standards, still quite well off. This altruism may not be racist, but it still arguably offends the moral ideal of impartiality. Further problems stem from the self-sacrificial element bound up with the vernacular understanding of altruism. Consider the heroes who rescue children from the proverbial burning building or – an important real life case we consider in Chapter 4 – rescuers of Jews in Nazi Europe. Did such people have a duty to incur these risks? If they did not, then should they have displayed such heroism? If they did, then does altruism sometimes ask too much of us? If we believe that some sacrifice of one's own interests for others can be required then we need to know how much can reasonably be asked for.

Altruism is a general phenomenon that involves taking the interests of the other as one's own; it is often identified with the Golden Rule (present in many religious and ethical traditions as we shall shortly see) – do unto others as you would have them do unto you. The Golden Rule seems to identify altruism with morality, but it is far from clear whether acting from the golden rule is always moral. Hobbes endorsed the Golden Rule, but interpreted it egoistically: a person first decides how they want to be treated and then they treat others on this basis. How about the masochist, for example, or religious zealots, or others with peculiar tastes which they would like 'altruistically' to share with others. Altruism, to make the point a final time, is a fundamentally simple idea but (perhaps for that reason) its implications and its association with morality, are far from simple. Investigating altruism, may seem a bit like taking a sweater apart to see what it is made of, leaving us with all yarn and no sweater. In this book we shall do some of this unstitching, but in a way that tries to preserve what is left.

We shall consider altruism from a number of disciplinary perspectives since it is in the engagement between its moral meaning and these perspectives that the most interesting questions about altruism lie. Besides ethics, then, we shall explore the contributions of evolutionary biology, psychology, anthropology, economics and political science, to the study of altruism. All of these disciplines have advanced our understanding of the nature of altruism, even if some of them – in particular evolutionary biology and economics – have expressed some scepticism over whether it genuinely exists. In the remainder of this chapter we shall survey the history of altruism in moral thought. Although the term altruism is a nineteenth century one, the concept has a long pedigree. The historical excavation of altruism's meanings will reveal how different thinkers construed the relative value of altruism and egoism, and the relationship between altruism and morality in a diversity of ways. One important issue which affects the latter is whether we believe that when people act in altruistic and/or moral ways they are motivated principally by reasons or by their emotions. This is the subject of intense debate among ethicists, and we explore it in Chapter 2. As we shall see there, one's view of whether the needs of others are thought to provide reasons for action, or touch us in more empathetic ways, also influences our view of reciprocity (a concept closely related to altruism) and impartiality, the view that every person's interests count the same – we consider these too.

In Chapter 3, we examine whether humans engaged in evolutionary struggle can remain altruistic. At first blush, there is a tension between the other-regardingness which altruism involves and the 'survival of the fittest' which evolution forces upon us. Evolutionists of various stripes have developed sophisticated models to explain the abundant evidence we have that humans and other animals do engage in behaviour that puts others first. These models are suggestive, especially when they seek to explain the evolutionary and anthropological origins of morality, but ultimately we reject the evolutionary approach since it bypasses perhaps the most distinctive feature of altruism in human beings: a person's motivation to assist another.

Chapter 4 considers a discipline which does have motivation at its centre: social psychology. Most psychologists make similar assumptions about the self-interested roots of human behaviour, but some of the more interesting work in psychology investigates the kinds of personalities (or 'traits') and circumstances (or 'states') in which altruistic motives are engaged. Studies show that people like helping those like themselves. But in emergency situations, especially when it is not clear who should be doing the helping, individuals will go to enormous lengths to avoid aiding a stranger. Notwithstanding this, we also discuss the research on one of the most inspiring group of altruists there are, rescuers of Jews in Nazi Europe. We consider whether socialization and family background explains the enormous risks they took, or whether there is, as Kristen Monroe argues in her important book, *The Heart of Altruism* (1996), a distinct perspective on human social life that only altruists possess.

Chapter 5 begins by considering the contribution of economic thought to the study of altruism. Many economists make assumptions about the self-interested nature of individuals, though this has not prevented them from explaining why we exhibit altruism too. We argue, however, that this reveals more about theoretical weaknesses of the dominant rational choice model of individual behaviour that most of them work with than it does about the reality of social behaviour. After considering again ideas of reciprocity and exchange (closely related to altruism not just for economists, but also for early anthropologists, such as Malinowski and Mauss), the chapter examines in some detail the arguments for altruism found in Richard Titmuss's classic work of social policy, *The Gift Relationship* ([1970] 1997). Titmuss's work offers a powerful socialist-communitarian defence of the welfare state still of relevance today, though we argue that he is ambivalent over whether giving or exchange is at the heart of it. The chapter concludes by analysing whether states are avenues for altruism or, on the contrary, institutions which crowd out people's other-regarding motivations.

In the final chapter, we take up again the question of whether the evolutionary perspective is combinable with a genuinely moral altruism and argue that a basic tension remains. Moreover, much of the in-group altruism in contemporary social life is, we maintain, morally suspect just because the favour it bestows on one's own community is incompatible with the impartial demands of morality. We explore whether communitarian altruism, an antidote to the selfishness of today's market societies, is extendable to citizens and strangers, and express some scepticism over whether it is. Altruism and justice, we want to say, are two different ideas. The chapter concludes by taking up again Monroe's idea of an altruistic perspective. We argue that the altruistic perspective, which unites reasons and emotion, is a distinctive view of human life and of morals and one which we ought to try to cultivate. We offer some small scale examples of how this might be achieved. Altruism, we conclude, though it has a more limited role in social life than many would like, remains fundamental for a human future.

Aristotelian and religious altruism

Altruism and morals have an intertwined history. Aristotle, with whom (together with Plato) so many moral questions start, certainly had a conception of something that looks much like altruism. This occurs in his discussion of friendship. Friendship, for Aristotle, contains components of altruism in that it is a relationship where one wishes good for one's friend for their sake (Aristotle 1976: 452). Aristotle was interested in whether good men act for the benefit of others or for themselves. This is a question about people's motives in ethical behaviour, of course, but it is also about the objects of our behaviour: self or other. Aristotle recognizes that people often seek to benefit their friends but also to benefit themselves. Selfishness, he goes on to point out, in the *Nichomachean Ethics*, is often treated as an attribute of the bad man (Aristotle 1976: 454). But things are not so simple, because in acting in a way that is motivated by the interests of one's friends one is acting both for the friend's sake and, by an extension of one's feeling, for oneself. Each person is, Aristotle thought, a sort of friend to themselves, and thus he blurs the distinction so central today between self and other. (He is not concerned with our obligations to strangers, something simply beyond his moral purview.)

Aristotle draws a distinction between self-love that is virtuous and self-love that is contrary to virtue, such as pure self-gratification. The pursuit of virtue involves developing oneself as a virtuous person: in acting (as we would term it) altruistically so as to benefit one's friends, a person promotes virtue in themselves and so becomes a better person. But if even altruism has a concern for self at its centre, the question arises of whether it is genuinely possible to be motivated solely out of a regard for the other's interests? According to Aristotle: 'It is true to say of the man of good character that he performs many actions for the sake of his friends and his country and if necessary even dies for them. For he will sacrifice both money and honours and in general the goods that people struggle to obtain in pursuit of what is morally fine' (Aristotle 1981: 456). In this passage Aristotle shows us that virtuous (altruistic) action does not merely benefit one's friends. As we shall see later on, one could do that on a whim or caprice. Virtuous action is rational moral action in pursuit of that which, in addition to the good it does its beneficiaries (one's friends), is also 'morally fine'. How the former motive relates to the latter one is an interesting question.

Part of the ethical tradition of both Judaism and Christianity is the importance of promoting the interests of the other, expressed in terms of the love of one's neighbour. For both traditions, this is an important point of departure for moral behaviour. The commandment in Leviticus to 'love thy neighbour as thyself' was written as a command against revenge (Leviticus, ch.19, v.18); and expands on the commandment not to covet one's neighbours' possessions or give false testimony against one's neighbour (Exodus, ch.20, v.16–7). These commandments amount to an ethic of how one ought to treat others in a manner that secures their interests, but they also relate to one's own perception of how one would want to be treated, and thus they involve ideas of reciprocity (to which we shall return). This eventually became known as the Golden Rule. In the Jewish rabbinic tradition, the phrase the 'Golden Rule' is not thought to have come into use until the eighteenth century, but it originates in the *Talmud*:

> A certain heathen came to Shammai and said to him: 'Make me a proselyte, on condition that you teach me the whole Torah while I stand on one foot'. Thereupon he repulsed him with the rod which was in his hand. When he went to Hillel, he said to him, 'what is hateful to you do not do to your neighbour: that is the whole Torah; all the rest of it is commentary; go and learn'.
>
> (*Talmud*, Shabbat, 31a)

In Matthew and Luke, the Golden Rule is given in positive terms as, 'Do unto others as you would have them do unto you' (Matthew, ch.7, v.12; Luke, ch.6, v.31). In the gospels, Jesus, addressing his disciples at the last supper exhorts them to: 'Love one another as I have loved you. No one has greater love than this than to lay down one's life for one's friends' (John, ch.15, v.12–3), which is repeated in John, ch.3, v.16. Here again, as in Aristotle, we have the ultimate expression of love for another in terms of being prepared to sacrifice one's life.

In the Judeo-Christian tradition, the phenomenon of altruism involves taking the interests of another as the goal of one's actions, not only in relation to the expression of love of another human being, but also as an expression of love to God, so 'the other' involves the Divine as well. It must be noted that the Golden Rule is not unique to this tradition, but is found in many other religions as well. For example, the Hindu *Mahabharata* holds that: 'One should not behave towards others in a way which is disagreeable to oneself. This is the essence of morality. All other activities are due to selfish desire' (*Mahabharata, Asusanasa Parva*, 113.8). Confucianism instructs each person to: 'Try your best to treat others as you would wish to be treated yourself, and you will find that this is the shortest way to benevolence' (*Mencius,* VII.A.4).

In the medieval period, Aquinas explored Aristotelian thought on virtue, where in addition to the Christian ethic of charity, courage was an important component too in pursuing happiness and the good in being virtuous (Aquinas 1964: II–II.129.2). Indeed, as Jordan points out, for Aquinas there is no virtue without charity since the highest human end is supernatural and cannot be realized without charity (Jordan 1993: 242). This is especially the case when one is confronted with the need to perform an act that is likely to endanger oneself physically or harm other things that one values. However, this kind of action is only virtuous if the actor reflects upon the danger or risk involved in the act. The spontaneous act is not praiseworthy (Aquinas 1964: II–II.123.1.2). The elements of risk and danger in virtuous action are components of that certain kind of altruistic action that is defined by sacrifice or by the need for the agent to give something up in performing the act. This action is, for Aquinas, directed ultimately towards the end of achieving divinity.

He assumes that with the love of charity, the truly courageous direct their intentions, both proximate and remote, to God (Aquinas 1964: II–II.123.7; I–II.65.2). He assumes that with the benefit of the Holy Spirit's gift of courage they act confidently and without fear, certain that they will finish whatever difficult work they begin and mindful of the insignificance of the goods they put at risk when compared to the everlasting they hope to achieve (Aquinas 1964: II–II.139.1; Bowlin 1999).

Having everlasting life or divinity as an end again brings into question the motivational state of the agent in understanding the nature of altruism. A common criticism of Christian altruism is that it is not really altruistic at all. The action is performed with the primary motivation coming from the possibility of reward of everlasting life. At any rate, altruism was certainly not yet understood in the way we think of it today.

Thomas Hobbes: egoism and its critics

In the mid-1600s, Thomas Hobbes argued for a view of human nature starkly at odds with moralities centred on other-regarding behaviour. The tradition of natural law which dominated the work of Aquinas and the scholastic tradition continued for other scholars, and is evident in some of Hobbes writing, but Hobbes's main aim was to appeal to intellect and reason as the foundation of morality. According to Hobbes, there was no transcendent normative order; rather humans had to create their own order to suit their biological and psychological natures. Political society was structured by the individualist need for survival. Hobbes' empiricist theory of morality presented humans as motivated by self-interest, stemming from his view of humans constantly striving to satisfy their own selfish desires, of which the main desire was, of necessity, survival.

Hobbes retained some notion of natural law, which for him amounted to the ability to exercise freedom in placing one's own interests above that of another, thus generating competition and the opportunity for exploitation. To prevent this outcome, Hobbes argued that human beings, despite being governed by subjective preferences and their own self-interest would, through means–ends reasoning, recognize certain common interests. These, he believed, would be adopted in order for individuals to maximize their own security. Thus Hobbes arrived at a list of natural laws, of which the last was, interestingly enough, the Golden Rule. 'The Lawes of Nature therefore need not any publishing nor Proclamation; as being contained in this one Sentence, approved by all the world, *Do not that to another, which thou thinketh unreasonable to be done by another to thy selfe*' (Hobbes [1651]

1996: 109). In contrast to Christian ethicists, for whom the Golden Rule was altruistic, Hobbes grounded it in the overriding need to secure one's own interests. It is questionable whether this is an expression of altruism. This is because the motivational reasons why people act so as to treat another's interests as their own in Hobbes's Golden Rule is quite different from that than in earlier treatments. When read in the context of the preceding laws of nature, the emphasis is on how I would want to be treated rather than how I treat the other. One treats the other person in order to elicit (on grounds of reciprocity) one's preferred treatment from them. Hobbes's view is thus thoroughly egoistic. This is evident from his definition of a law of nature; it is a rule according to which a person is forbidden to do anything that is self-destructive or removes their ability to preserve their own life (Hobbes [1651] 1996: 91). The negative aspect of the expression is different from the Biblical expression, reading 'do not that to another', rather than 'do unto others'. In other words, do not do anything to others that you wouldn't want done to you; the things that you would have done to you being those things that secure your own survival. It is a rule that is to be understood in the context of the overriding goal of securing one's own interests. The Golden Rule can therefore be read as the expression of a reciprocal ethic rather than a purely altruistic one.

Hobbes' egoism was opposed by Richard Cumberland, who wanted to return the ethics of natural law back to the Christian tradition. Cumberland believed that Hobbes made an error in his assumption that the object of every person's will is what one thinks is good for themselves. Hobbes presumes that everyone pursues their own good, and that justice and peace are accidental pursuits (Cumberland 1672). In other words, according to Cumberland, Hobbes fails to recognize the pursuit of good for the sake of others, a good that is not self-directed. In Hobbes's theory it is only accidental that peace and justice emerge in the securing of good for oneself. Cumberland's own view supports a view of human nature where reason, understood in a substantive sense, is central, and where morality is grounded in human rational abilities, rather than the emotions. For Cumberland, the rational gives rise to the moral, which for him was understood as the discovery of the laws of nature.

Samuel Pufendorf wrote a more detailed defence of an altruistic attitude towards others following on from Cumberland, in his

'The Duty of Man and Citizen', in which the human tendency towards selfish behaviour is counteracted by human social living where various duties to others are to be upheld. These included, under the specific heading of 'Common duties of Humanity', the duty:

> that every man promote the advantage of the other, so far as he conveniently can. For since nature has established a kind of kinship among men, it would not be enough to have refrained from injuring or despising others; but we must also bestow such attentions upon others – or mutually exchange them – that thus mutual benevolence may be fostered among men. Now we benefit others either definitely or indefinitely, and that with a loss or else without loss to ourselves.
>
> (Pufendorf [1673] 1991: bk.I, ch.VIII)

Here we have a clear expression of altruism, combining ideas of taking the interests of the other as one's own, together with the idea of mutual aid and, more significantly, together with the likelihood that taking others' interests as one's own will involve some cost to oneself.

Christian Wolff, whose 1738 work, *Philosophia Practica Universalis* was referred to by Kant in the *Groundwork to the Metaphysics of Morals* (Kant [1785] 1996: 46), held that duties towards others were the same as duties towards oneself, an idea that not only revisits the expression of the Golden Rule as it appears in the Gospels, but also St. John's exhortation that one is to love others as oneself (Wolff 1720: 796). Wolff emphasizes the obligation to help those who are in need, insofar as one is capable of doing so, what they are limited by their situation and ability. This duty does not extend to putting oneself in danger. Wolff expresses this clearly in his reflections on rendering assistance. The ethic of the good Samaritan, however praiseworthy, does not extend to failing to meet the duties one owes to one's self:

> The utility of these rules is great and extensive. For through them we can judge in all cases whether or not we are obligated to help someone. For example we see a man on the road that has been attacked by a robber, who is robbing him and trying to kill him. We are by nature

fearful and weak and, consequently unfit to protect anyone. We must therefore be aware that if we intervened we would not save the victim but we would be put in danger with him. Because we as well as the other are obligated to avoid all danger to life, and it is not in our power to run to his aid, we are not obligated to do so. One obligation cannot be opposed by another.

(Wolff 1720: 772)

For Wolff, sacrificial altruism has its limits, a stipulation which to a modern reader is perfectly sensible. Furthermore, although Wolff promotes the obligation of a person to love others as they love themselves, he insists on an unequal distribution of this love: 'Works of love are called benefits, and accordingly friends strive to benefit us. Because we are obligated to love all men as ourselves, we owe most love to those who benefit us. The love of the benefactor is called gratitude, and so we should be grateful to our benefactor' (Wolff 1720: 834). This bias towards benefactors introduces, among other difficulties, the question of what one ought to do if a stranger's need is more pressing than that of a benefactor, a viewpoint which raises problems for more impartial understandings of morality and justice.

Immanuel Kant pays compliment to Wolff's contribution to ethics, noting at the beginning of *the Groundwork to the Metaphysics of Morals* that the idea of a universal practical philosophy, which he sought to defend, had already been formulated by Wolff. In *the Groundwork*, Kant sets out to find a justification for morality grounded in reason. He does this through a complex argument that shows the possibility of a fundamental universal principle for morality, called the categorical imperative. This imperative, he maintained, was the 'supreme principle of morality' (Kant [1785] 1996: 47), and it was expressed in several forms in *the Groundwork*. Kant sought to trace the motive for pure moral behaviour in a way which avoided reliance on empirical sources, such as feelings or desires. The latter, however, includes much of what we today would consider to be involved in altruistic behaviour.

Kant considered acting to benefit others in need as a moral duty and in *the Groundwork* he introduces beneficence (doing good to others) as an example of a categorical morality, universally binding on all rational agents. In Kant's terms, this means that all rational beings would agree to the principle that one has a moral duty to be beneficent to others. Beneficence was a moral duty because humans can find themselves in a position where they require assistance from others who have the capacity to help. The rationale behind acting according to the duty of beneficence is that it would be irrational to adopt non-beneficence towards others as a universal principle, as this would mean that such an individual ought to be willing to forgo help from others when they themselves are in a position of need. It is important to note that Kant's position gives moral reason a central role in motivation. This contrasts strongly with the approach taken by the empiricist tradition, where it is accepted that human sentiment has normative force; reason, in other words, can motivate us to act, right moral values are expressed in and through our acting. We will return to this contrast below when we look at the notion of motivation.

The empiricist tradition and early evolutionary thought

The development of the empiricist tradition in England saw the ethics of love for one's neighbour that came through the Christian tradition meet the ethics of emotion, on the one hand, and a rational ethics on the other. We have already encountered empiricism in Hobbes where the fear of death and a means–ends conception of reasoning were together a non-metaphysical basis for the foundation of political society. This meeting led to a new understanding of morality and – important for our purposes – altruistic morality. This was expressed by Lord Shaftesbury (1977) for example, who held that morality was a development of feeling and, following him, Hutcheson who believed that humans had a moral sense, which involved the use of sentiment rather than reason in producing moral judgements. This new way of thinking about morality, in terms of emotions, brought it closer to altruistic concerns.

Hume, developing his moral theory from Hutcheson, argued that sentiment was the basis of moral judgement. Hume devoted a substantial part of his *Enquiry Concerning the Principles of Morals* to the subject of benevolence, providing from the outset a collection of terms associated with this moral sentiment which he thought expressed 'the highest merit which human nature is capable of attaining' (Hume [1777] 1975: 176). The terms he cites are all forms of virtue: sociability, good naturedness, humaneness, mercifulness, gratitude, friendliness, generosity and beneficence. It is the last of these, beneficence, which reflects altruism most clearly and (as we saw) is significant for Kant as well. Hume saw the origins of moral sentiments as emerging through familial and other social relationships. It was here that humans cultivated the feelings of sympathy which were central to motivating moral action. It was sympathy, according to Hume, that allowed a person to transfer feelings from one person onto another. (Hume [1739–40] 1888: 493). This emphasis on emotion is important for the development of altruism, as it provides a different account of the source of motivation. Rather than reason, it is emotion and sentiment that provide the appropriate foundation for altruistic morality. This position has been supported more recently by Lawrence Blum, whom we will consider in the next chapter. Important, too, is the relationship between emotion and sentiment. Michael Ruse, an evolutionary ethicist, considers Hume's views on the origins of human morality to be very close to Darwin's. We will look at this in Chapter 3.

The eighteenth century Scottish economist and philosopher Adam Smith, a friend of Hume's, took a very different view. Like Hobbes, he believed that egoism helped advance the common good. Specifically, if each person was allowed to pursue their own economic freedom, and thus advance their own interests, there would be a substantial economic gain overall and that general welfare would therefore be served. However, Smith considered Hobbes' strict egoistic view of human nature to be overstated and argued, in *The Theory of Moral Sentiments*, that: 'How selfish soever man may be supposed, there are evidently some principles in his nature which interest him in the fortune of others and render their happiness necessary to him, though he derives nothing from it, except the pleasure of seeing it' (Smith [1790] 2002: 11). Thus Smith, like Hume, accepts that morality is grounded in sympathy, though as Maris points out, Smith interpreted sympathy as the ability of a person to imagine themselves in someone else's position, whereas Hume saw sympathy as the principle by which it is possible for a person to transfer feelings to another person (Maris: 1981: 59).

However, Smith was aware that it is our own feelings we are imagining rather than the other person's. Imagining oneself in the position of another does not necessarily lead to acting on that imagining. For example, if I see someone experience pain, such as twisting an ankle, I may imagine what that pain is like for me to experience when I sympathize with the sufferer. One might think that more than this is needed for a genuinely altruistic response, namely, taking another's interests as one's own and acting from another's perspective. Maris argues that Smith distinguishes between altruism, which he regards as an uneven emotion involving only those in close proximity, and other moral feelings which are more equally distributed and allow objectification. The latter are involved in moral phenomena, such as putting oneself in another's place or meeting one's duty in action towards another. Altruism, for Smith, expressed as self-sacrifice, is directed to those who are close to us, and this is not the same as putting oneself in the position of another. The latter involves moral feeling and sympathy which is stronger than 'the feeble spark of benevolence' (Smith [1790] 2002: 156). The stronger aspect involves reason-principle conscience and the perspective of an impartial observer, rather than the love of one's neighbour.

Although altruism as a term was not in use at this time, it is interesting to note that the very characteristics of what one might consider to be an idea of altruism were held by Smith to be motivations involving reason and conscience: strong and reliable moral feelings that Smith does not associate with self-sacrifice. The source of other-regarding behaviour is not to be found in benevolence. These ideas mainly concern the problem of being able to take another person's interest as one's own and be motivated to act in a way that benefits the other, crucial ideas in any understanding of altruism. What is important, moreover, about the moral philosophies of Hobbes, Shaftesbury, Hutcheson, Hume and Smith is that, although they have differing perspectives on individuals' motivation, they all reject the idea, maintained by Kant among others, that morality has rational grounds. They therefore provide an intellectual setting for the emergence of the evolutionary approach to morality that was to come.

Auguste Comte

The meaning of altruism developed its content in the Jewish and, especially, the Christian tradition of ethics. It subsequently focused on the individual's ability to be the source of altruistic motivation as empiricism came into its own. The more specific modern meaning, however, appears in Auguste Comte, who was responsible for coining the term *'altruisme'* to refer to benevolent and sympathetic feelings that, according to him, ought to be promoted in place of more selfish ones. Whereas in the moral philosophical tradition, consideration of others included duties to God, to the community and to oneself, Comte wished to see ethics develop only out of our social relationships. Altruism was centrally about promoting other people's interests, and morality was the triumph of altruism over egoism. Comte saw the origins of sympathy, socialization and altruism, in the animal world. With the emergence in the mid-nineteenth century of a science of the brain, Comte also believed that sympathy and altruism could be shown to originate from specific areas of the brain.

The egoistic sentiments that are needed for survival were seen by Comte as stronger than the weaker altruistic and social capacities. These weaker capacities could, however, be strengthened through education; in the course of human evolution altruistic functions in the brain had became stronger and capable of controlling egoistic passions (Maris 1981). This view of the relationship between the egoistic instincts and altruistic tendencies meant that the goal of living for others in human social evolution was problematic; the capacities for intellect and altruism had to overcome the requirements of self-preservation. The reasons Comte develops to support this view are difficult and complex. He held that in the course of human evolution the natural predominance and supremacy of instinct is sacrificed to the higher development of reason. This brings about a 'fatal separation' between heart and mind that threatens the unity of man. Any attempt to separate altruism from egoism and promote only altruism would be disastrous for society, unless it had reached the requisite stage of development. If it had not, it would be difficult to distinguish a pure altruism from an altruism that helped promote the egoism of others (Comte [1852] 1966: vol. 1, para. 66).

The family was where altruism was first learnt and practised, a crucible for its subsequent transformation into a fully fledged moral and social phenomenon. However, although this is the first location of altruism, it is not fully developed in the family. Only later, and with a certain amount of abstraction, can altruism be pursued as a universal goal of humanity. This stage of moral development in society had not yet been reached, according to

Comte; it would do so through education and the continued co-operation between the intellect and altruistic feelings. The result is a civilization that is, in general, characterized by the continuous removal of all personal (self-interested) and egocentric tendencies, and one which adopts altruism as the behaviour that cements social relationships.

There is a move, then, from the level of the individual to the family that was the focus of both the Kantian and the empiricist view, where altruistic tendencies were thought to function as a foundation for living in society (Comte [1852] 1966: vol. 3, para. 69). Eventually, thought Comte, a spontaneous, natural, innate altruism (Comte [1851] 1969–70: vol. 3, para. 589; vol. 4, para. 20) would come about, as human beings, through the evolution of thought, were able to assert the superiority of intellect over emotion, and altruism over egoism in their inclinations. This development is, according to Comte, 'less easy to realise than the egotistical unity', because of the effort required by the intellect and is therefore, once arrived at, 'superior to wealth and stability' (Comte [1852] 1966: vol. 2, para. 9) in making human social relationships secure. The evolution of altruism involves the subordination of self-love to meeting the needs of others, and this is a source of well-being for the individual as well as for society at large. Altruism is only able to operate successfully in the face of a strong egoistic instinct when it works hand in hand with human rational capacity. This capacity provides a rational insight into social negotiation, where the rational encounters human needs. On its own, intellect and rationality lead to vanity, but when encountering human needs in the social context, the intellect is put to use to serve human needs, serving this best through the practice of altruism (Comte [1852] 1966: vol. 1, para. 700; vol. 2, para. 204). This evolved altruistic morality that Comte saw as becoming universal to all humanity.

Herbert Spencer expressed similar thoughts on altruism to Comte, apart from the fact that, in the context of increasing interest in Darwinian ideas on natural selection, Spencer looked on evolution as a physical process. Social Darwinism, introduced into the intellectual landscape by Spencer, read Darwin's theories of natural selection as a way in which the evolutionary process could involve the moral betterment of human beings through the development of altruism, followed by its disappearance as it became redundant. Spencer avoided the radical approach of

Comte, since he believed that Comte's pure, familial altruism would lead down a path to an individual's ever increasing dependence on the community, this being contrary to his stress on the individual as the motor of human evolution. Spencer's approach, unlike Comte's, was individualist and Spencer regarded egoism as having priority over altruism. 'That egoism precedes altruism in order of imperativeness is evident. For the acts that make continued life possible, must, on the average be more peremptory than all those acts which life makes possible, including the acts that benefit others' (Collins 1895: ch.11, sec.68).

Egoism and its related acts, in being peremptory, provide an imperative demanding compliance with those forces that make the continuation of life possible. Spencer defined altruism simply as action that benefits others instead of benefiting oneself. He presented a utilitarian form of altruism that can be seen as coming through the English empirical tradition in moral philosophy, having as its predecessor a restricted egoism (Spencer 1879: ch. 1, para. 69; 1872: chs. 1, 7, 9). For Spencer, pure egoism and pure altruism are harmful to man in that they do not secure the utilitarian aim of the greatest happiness. The principle of loving one's neighbour as oneself, he argued, requires one to be simultaneously egoistic and altruistic – the willingness to receive injury to self for the other's benefit and the expectation that the other accepts benefits at the cost of injury to others leads to traits that Spencer thought could not co-exist (Collins 1895: bk. XII. sec.82–9). The commitment to self-sacrifice, which altruism involved, is incompatible with Spencer's commitment to the survival of the fittest in his evolutionary theory. The strength exhibited by the egoist allows superior organisms to progress biologically. Altruism is beneficial, though, because of what it gives socially in aiding reproductive success through social life, it is important in economic relationships and provides humans with pleasure. Ultimately egoism and altruism are to be reconciled to one another in the process of human evolution.

The conflict between egoism and altruism is, however, only transitional and eventually, according to Spencer, they became more harmoniously related, as in the industrial society where each person works for all, and when the individual's needs and interests coincide with the laws of the market. Evolution was the principle behind Spencer's social philosophy, and he believed that man would adapt fully to his social situation since he would be eradicated if he did not keep pace. Eventually, altruism would no longer be necessary, because, in the perfect community all are simultaneously required to maintain themselves and to fulfil completely all the obligations on which the community is based in order to keep it in good working order (Spencer 1879: ch.1, para. 80). Altruism becomes obsolete because the needs of the individual are most fully realized in a society where self-interest coincides with the interests of all. Altruism here is still a 'sympathetic pacification which each receives as a free addition to their egoistic pleasures' (Spencer 1879: ch.1, para. 98), for example, in the bringing up of young by the family, altruism reverts to taking pleasure in other people's happiness.

From Nietzsche to some modern views on altruism

Nietzsche criticized Spencer's evolutionary theory heavily, together with the British empiricist tradition, referring to social Darwinists as 'these English psychologists'. Of them, he states: 'The way they have bungled their moral genealogy comes to light at the very beginning where the task is to investigate the origin of the concept and judgement "good"' (Nietzsche [1910] 1992: 461). Nietzsche saw neither altruism nor the development of social relationships as a levelling co-operation system in which the meaning of human development could be found, but rather looked to the individual. He was particularly interested in altruism for he saw it as a psychological weakness in human beings. Altruism, for Nietzsche, was the most hypocritical form of egoism, grounded in resentment of others' success (Nietzsche [1901] 1968). The altruistic person used their own low self-worth to measure the value of others' activities (Nietzsche [1901] 1968).

Nietzsche encountered altruism through Spencer's hypothesis, which treated human beings as the most advanced Darwinian animal, able to cope with the demands of altruism and egoism in a skilful manner. Spencer's altruism, which keeps an element of egoism in place, is also read by Nietzsche as coming from the Judeo-Christian tradition. Nietzsche condemns it because of what it brings about: the removal of the self at the expense of an obsession with the other. This critical perspective on morality is contained in his resentment thesis in *The Genealogy of Morals*, but he also explicitly criticizes altruism elsewhere. In his essay 'Daybreak', Nietzsche sees the cause of altruism in the poetic interest of those who have lacked the experience of love and thus construct a mistaken idolized context in which this love can occur (Nietzsche [1881] 1982: bk. II, para. 147). He sees the individual who is *'unegoistic'* as one who 'is hollow and wants to be full' or 'one who is overfull and wants to be emptied – both go in search of an individual who will serve their purpose' (Nietzsche [1881] 1982: bk. II, para. 145), which is to find a love that is unegoistic. For Nietzsche, the tendency to think of others and not oneself comes from a sense of pity. The interest in someone else's plight or in their suffering is motivated by an unconscious reflection on what our own suffering would be. On rescuing behaviour he writes: 'Let us reflect seriously upon this question: why do we leap after someone who has fallen into the water in front of us, even though we feel no kind of affection for him? Out of pity: at that moment we are thinking only of the other person' (Nietzsche [1881] 1982: bk. II, para. 133). But if we reflect upon this at a deeper level, according to Nietzsche, we will see that our action is really motivated by self-interest even if we may not be conscious of this at the time. We act to help a person in need in order to relieve ourselves of the feeling of pity: 'But it is only this suffering of our own which we get rid of when we perform deeds of pity' (Nietzsche [1881] 1982: bk. II, para. 133). Nietzsche is starkly opposed to altruism and any other morality that involves taking the other as the focus of an action over and above the self.

Max Scheler supported Nietzsche's resentment thesis in terms of contemporary values, but opposed Nietzsche's historical reading of Christianity as being rooted in resentment (Schroeder 2000). According to Scheler, the love of others, that the Christian perspective is interested in, flows from their own life force; man loves the other not for their own ends or out of weakness, but because of positive values. Altruists end up fleeing from the fear of self and view themselves as less worthy (Scheler 1954). This is because, according to Scheler, altruism cannot answer the question: why am I or why will I not be worthy of a positive value of love from the other? In other words, it does not comprehend the value of reciprocation.

Modern ideas of altruism have taken two different courses after the advent of evolutionary theory. First, in evolutionary thought the term has been used to refer to some specific consequences of animal behaviour, ignoring the intentions or the motivations behind it. Second, altruism has remained a term applied to other-regarding behaviour, ranging from the self-sacrificial to merely the taking on of others' ends as one's own. The latter, as we have seen, has a long history in moral philosophy. There is considerable debate over both these positions. The latter view, where the motive and intention are of importance are of particular interest to us in this book, but we shall consider the evolutionary perspective (in Chapter 3) too, as it informs many current debates.

Through this survey of the phenomenon of altruism, not only has it become evident that there are multiple understandings of the term, but the phenomenon of promoting the value of others has been of some considerable moment in the history of ideas. The question of the meaning of altruism has arisen in many contexts and against a background of quite different views of human beings. A key divide seems to be the question of whether humans are altruists by virtue of their use of reason or through their emotions.

2

Altruism, motives and morality

We saw in the historical overview of altruism, in ethical thought, that the issue of motivation was quite central. It is important, for both moral philosophers and the rest of us, to consider whether we act altruistically because of desires and sentiments or on the basis of reason (or perhaps both). For one thing, answering this question may better inform us on whether people are genuinely altruistic or ultimately selfish, the latter rendering pure altruism impossible. As we shall see, considering the question of motivation leads us into some difficult and longstanding debates in moral philosophy. In this chapter we begin by setting out the more rationalistic position, whose greatest proponent is Kant, and then we outline the more emotive position, defended recently by Lawrence Blum who draws in turn on David Hume. We side with a modified version of the former view, in part because altruistic emotions seem themselves to involve reason. The chapter goes on to examine three further ways that morality challenges altruism: whether we have a duty to be altruistic; whether reciprocity is genuinely altruistic; and, the relationship between altruism and impartiality.

Reasons as motives

What does it mean to say that people are motivated by reason? Kant's view relies on a person's acceptance of the *categorical imperative* as rationally binding them to a course of action – and providing the source of their motivation. The categorical imperative is his general moral principle: 'Act only in accordance with that maxim through which you can at the same time will that it become a universal law' (Kant [1797] 1996: 421). A maxim is a principle of action. We can take a maxim, such as 'it is good to give money to the poor' and test by the categorical imperative to see if it is rationally binding on all human beings. If it is, then we have reason for accepting it as a moral duty for all to perform: in this case, everyone would have a reason to give money to the poor.

In Kant's writings, the duty of beneficence is the closest example of reasoning that leads to altruistic behaviour that can be rationally motivated. Kant distinguishes between beneficence and benevolence. There is a slight difference in meaning between them, but an important one. Beneficence (*Wohltun* in Kant's words) is understood as doing good; benevolence (*Wohlwollen*) is understood merely as wishing good. It is thus only beneficence that relates directly to action. Kant further defines beneficence as benevolence manifest in the practical love of humans. So a duty to be beneficent involves from the outset *acting* on an obligation, not just recognizing it at a theoretical level. A benevolent person takes satisfaction in the happiness of others, but beneficence is defined more specifically by Kant as 'the maxim of making other's happiness one's end' (Kant [1797] 1996: 452). Though he favours the terminology of beneficence, Kant offers here a clear expression of altruism. However, he has not yet shown that we have a duty to be altruistic (Scott 2004).

Kant argues that we do have a duty to be altruistic through asking us to imagine a peculiar situation of someone of great prosperity and success (Kant [1797] 1996: 423–4). This wealthy person is also aware that others are not rich and in fact lack the things they need. Furthermore, he knows that he can act so as to help those in need. However, in Kant's illustration, this individual person is not disposed to give assistance. He expresses his contentment with the status quo, by saying 'let everyone be as happy as heaven pleases or as he can make himself' (Kant [1797] 1996: 423–4). This attitude may seem (to the prosperous man, not to us) rather generous. He does not wish anyone harm, and wishes to promote individual freedom and personal space. 'I will take nothing from him [the pauper] nor envy him', he says (Kant [1797] 1996: 423–4). Even though he recognizes the needy person's position, he has simply decided not to contribute to their welfare; he is entirely indifferent to it.

Now we must imagine if the principle of non-beneficence were adopted as a universal law – or maxim of action – for every person. Kant concedes that if everyone adopted such a principle the 'human race might well subsist' (Kant [1797] 1996: 423). Indeed, he says that a sincere and committed egoism would lead to a better state of affairs than if others were occasionally sympathetic, but also deceitful, unpredictable and liable to act on a whim. However, though we can entertain the possibility of the wealthy man who does nothing, Kant insists that it is impossible that we could wish such a maxim as a universal law. We would never, he maintains, give our rational consent to such egoism as a maxim of universal validity to be practised by everyone. A person who willed consistent selfish behaviour of the kind that recognized distress in others, but did nothing about it, would place themselves in a contradictory position. Their avowed beliefs would be at odds with *their* possible need of help in the future from others. An agent who adopted, as a law of action, a consistent unresponsiveness to the needs of others, would deprive themselves of any hope that others might help them meet their own future needs. Only if people were so independent that they had no needs that others could help in meeting (not contingently but as an unconditional truth), could they possibly adopt this maxim as a universal law. What Kant is challenging is the inability of any human to be independent in this way.

Kant assumes that humans are not disposed to living in isolation from others, or even capable of living such a life. No one can satisfy their goals, aspirations and needs in solitude, and hence it would be irrational to adopt universal non-beneficence as a law. This seems fairly uncontentious. We need help and assistance from others and altruism is an important component of this. It is interesting here that Kant in his political writings recognizes a psychological tension in human behaviour, which may be familiar to the reader's experience: people often desire both solitude and sociability. When in the company of others we seek solitude and when in solitude we long for the company of others. The origins of morality and altruism may have developed as a response to this tension in social organization, trying to deal with this predicament of being pulled in different directions. Despite the option of pursuing independence from others, our recognition that we too are needy beings, helps define some of the physical and social limits of human existence.

We still need to know how weighty the duty is to be altruistic. After all, there is virtually no limit to the altruism we could perform for others, we could abjectly sacrifice our own interests at every turn, even to the extent that it led to our own death. Fortunately Kant does not believe such a demand is a reasonable one. The duty of beneficence, he believes, is meritorious and imperfect. By classing it an imperfect duty, Kant means there is no strict *requirement* to be altruistic, as there are cases where it is not possible to be so, and cases where the duty to be altruistic is outweighed by other concerns. A meritorious duty is one where an agent is not morally blameworthy if they fail to perform (Kant [1797] 1996: 454). It may well be a good thing to give my money to the poor, but I cannot be required to give away all my money as this would place me in a needy position. I may be confronted with a drowning person but if I cannot swim, I cannot be under a moral obligation to save them. Our abilities and the circumstances in which we find ourselves set limits on how altruistic (beneficent) we can be expected to be.

Kant's argument for beneficence is embedded within his rationalistic framework, where human beings are conceived of as having the capacity to set goals, arrive at principles to reach those goals and freely choose to act on those principles. It may appear difficult to get a grip on the whole of Kant's framework, but its important element concerns the nature of choice. In order to choose we must be able to reason and Kant regards reason as practical, not just theoretical (Kant [1797] 1996: 412). Crucially, our power of choice as human beings is manifested not only in choosing which ends we prefer and which goals we want to pursue, but also in being able to act contrary to the direction our emotions lead us if we are required to do so by duty. A good illustration of struggles of choice are displayed by Homer Simpson in the long running US television cartoon. Those familiar with the series will recognize that Homer is a character constantly torn by wanting to follow his desires and choosing more worthy goals. More often than a competition between alternate desires, Homer experiences a struggle between desire and reason.

James Lawler (1999) captures this well in an analysis of Homer's predicament where he must choose between going fishing or attempting to save his marriage from failure. The location at which marriage counselling is offered is near a lake and Homer is caught between the opportunity to catch the 'Great Sherman' catfish or to resolve to rescue his marriage. He plumps for the latter, but later attempts to sneak out of the counselling to go fishing, only to be caught by his wife, Marge. He renounces his ways and goes for a walk to reflect on his selfishness, but after a while he finds a lost fishing rod and when he tugs on the line, he accidentally ends up with it snaring a huge fish that turns out to be the Great Sherman. Lawler interprets the ensuing struggle between Homer and the fish as a struggle of wills, a metaphor for Homer's internal struggle. Having eventually caught the fish and having the prospect of fame ahead, he is confronted by Marge again. Faced with a choice between selfish desire and moral duty 'Homer renounces fishing celebrity for family', declaring 'I gave up fame and breakfast for our marriage' (Lawler 1999: 149). The general point, to return to Kant, is that while an emotional state may hold someone back from being altruistic, or indeed from pursuing any morally worthwhile goal, reason *can*, in principle, motivate us to act. Reasons (as motives) for altruism can in principle override emotion and desire. A duty to behave altruistically means one has a powerful reason to do so, and it is the reason itself which prompts the act.

The rational commitment demanded by the principle of beneficence is that no one would rationally will that they live in a world where universal non-beneficence is practised. The extent to which we are social and needy beings rules us out from rationally consenting to such a state of affairs. Thus to will a world of non-beneficence would be to act contrary to reason. As humans we have needs we cannot forgo and moreover it is not possible to predict what our future needs may be. It would be irrational to act in a way that would deny the fulfilment of present and future needs.

Kant's argument that we have a duty to be altruistic grounded in reason seems to ignore some of the features we associate with an altruistic response to a situation, such as compassion, sympathy, fellow feeling, and so on. It is common to think that we act on such emotions when we act altruistically, especially when we respond immediately to what a situation demands – the most common way of acting in our daily lives. Furthermore, his notion of duty may seem unduly to restrict altruism: in situations where their altruism stems more from their feelings, then a person would not genuinely be moral, in Kant's view. A person who gives a lift to a friend out of kindness, behaves in neither a moral nor an altruistic way (although Kant would concede that this is a good act). Altruism, for Kant, seems a rather demanding virtue.

Contemporary moral philosophers have, however, followed his lead in explicating reason-based approaches to moral motivation. A good example is Thomas Nagel, in his well known *The Possibility of Altruism* (1970). Nagel sees altruism not as a kind of abject self-sacrifice, but simply as a willingness to act in the interests of other persons, without any ulterior motives. Altruism is 'any behaviour motivated merely by the belief that someone else will benefit or avoid harm by it' (Nagel 1970: 16). Importantly, Nagel holds that altruistic reasons themselves motivate action, and in doing so he rejects the view that altruism is a peculiar form of desire. Nagel's account follows Kant's in seeking *a priori* or metaphysical foundation for moral action. In a similar vein, Gewirth (1978) argues that there is a relationship between the reasons a person accepts and their pursuit of their own purposes. Gewirth's argument appeals to the fact that a desire, or judgement, that one ought to do something entails that one has reasons for actually *doing* that thing. The judgement that I ought to send money to disaster relief, for example, contains at a deeper level a reason for actually doing it. It is reason, therefore, and not simply desire, which does some motivational work. But given that people often do have compelling reasons for doing altruistic things which they do not in fact act upon, this approach faces a difficulty.

Altruism motivated by emotion

Our everyday understanding of altruism regards it as closely connected to compassion, sympathy and similar kinds of emotional experiences. People are altruistic for reasons, certainly, but also because of their feelings and allied psychological states outside the narrow Kantian moral framework. Altruism not motivated by rational requirements does not seem any less morally worthy for that. Lawrence Blum in his book *Friendship, Altruism and Morality* (1980) is highly critical of the Kantian approach to ethics for just this reason: it neglects the nuanced and subtle aspects of altruistic behaviour in humans. Specifically, Blum interprets Kant's position as consisting of three aims (all of which he goes on to contest). First, according to Blum, Kant wishes to articulate a single fundamental principle of morality that applies to all human beings – this is his categorical imperative. Second, Kant believes that our common human reason applied to moral knowledge must yield no internal tensions or contradictions as otherwise it would not give us a principled approach to morality. Finally, Blum interprets Kant's position as strict and categorical: moral obligation is unconditionally binding, on all people and at all times, just because it is the right thing to do. These three aspects do not fit well with how altruism or indeed morality is actually encountered in the world in which we live.

For Kant, human emotions are quite distinct from reason and rationality, and are typified by passivity. They are not in our control and we cannot be held responsible for them as they lie outside of the scope of the will. Feelings and emotions are transitory, changeable, capricious and weak, in that they are subject to mood and inclination. Since they are not chosen they cannot be the source of moral praise or blame. The Kantian view of altruistic emotions is that they arise in response to particular circumstances and do not have the generality and universality that is required by morality. They therefore involve bias, partiality in being responsive to non-moral and non-rational considerations, and are highly subjective, not to mention unreliable, inconsistent, unprincipled and irrational. For Kant, right moral judgement requires abstraction from feeling and emotion.

Blum, however, contests Kant's view that moral motives need to be reliable, consistent and not affected by inclination. He also disagrees with the idea that they cannot arise from contingent facts and predispositions of agents, or indeed that they must be non-egoistic. Acting from the motives of altruistic feelings and emotions, according to Blum, is to act from inclination and desire. These feelings and emotions are *egoistic* in that an agent has a particular inclination to promote the other's good, in order to satisfy their own desire. (This puts them into conflict with the important moral idea of impartiality, as we shall see.) Blum's position, then, is that altruism is a special kind of emotion. The advantage of his approach is that in accepting emotional sources of obligation he seems to provide us with a more complete picture of what altruism actually involves, one that is closer to our common moral experience.

In contrast to Kant's approach, Blum thinks that there are different types of goodness and that they do not all conform to a single, unitary principle. We cannot always reason consistently, and contradictions do – and should be permitted to – occur in moral systems. In fact, Blum's more open, pluralistic approach does not make any categorical distinctions between moral and non-moral standpoints. This is in large part because of the phenomenon of friendship, as well as the significance of compassion, sympathy and concern, which seem to cut across the distinction. Further, as we can rely on emotion to guide us towards altruistic action, we do not need a rational foundation to morality.

Altruism is defined by Blum as 'a regard for the good of another person for his own sake or conduct motivated by such regard' (Blum 1980: 9). It need not include any notion of self-sacrifice or self-neglect, but simply involves an agent being 'motivated by a genuine regard for another's welfare' (Blum 1980: 10). The only important distinction in morality for Blum is that between one's concern for others and one's concern for self, in other words between altruism and egoism. The altruistic emotion has a special status compared with other human emotions: it is intentional, meaning that it points to something outside the self. It also has a cognitive aspect in that our recognition of the fact that another person is in a state of need, and our assessment of the importance of this is not an abstract moral judgment but is constitutive of the emotion. Altruistic feelings are 'non-episodic' in that they continue over time and are not necessarily oriented to specific situations, such as being concerned about a particular person in a particular situation.

Blum's position owes much to that articulated by David Hume whom we considered when we considered the empiricist position in the last chapter. In his *Enquiry Concerning the Principles of Morals*, Hume takes the view that morality depends on '[s]ome sense or feeling which nature has made universal in the whole species' (Hume [1777] 1975: 173). The Slovak composer, Albert Albrechts, who devoted much of his time and resources to the care and education of children, nicely captures the role of sentiment together with the aesthetic in the interrelationship between altruism and creativity. This quotation is displayed in the Slovak National Museum of Music in Bratislava:

> The artistic can never be divided from the human. Our final aim is to perceive our culture as an everyday instinctive need, just as respect for others, understanding and altruism are the most beautiful content of our life. This is what matters. It is necessary to be brave, to be able to

think and to give your heart: it is necessary to know how to love. Whoever hates is bad, whoever loves is good. Whoever is bad, destroys, whoever is good builds. It is easy and quick to destroy something, but building is slow and difficult work! We have no more than this one life, so let us build so that after our death, people will be able to say something, which is rarely said by one another: 'It is a pity!' And let us do our work without stopping, while we have enough strength and youth, while it is day, because evening will come and we will no longer be able to work.

(Albrechts n.d.)

Some problems with Kant and Blum

That feelings and sentiments articulate certain elements of desire is unproblematic; the relationship between desire and morality, by contrast, is controversial, especially when we consider how morality is to serve human relationships satisfactorily. One can understand Kant's problem that grounding morality in human inclinations risks making it too contingent. However, this does not eliminate inclination from the processes of everyday moral decision-making and the motivations that power those processes. The Kantian position does not deny the role of human psychology in causing certain moral motivations; it says simply that grounding principles in these psychological facts must be avoided if our moral behaviour is to be reliable and consistent. The consistency of moral principles makes categorical demands on how we ought to act; whether we do so act, or are even convinced that we should do so, is another matter.

Blum clearly thinks that moral consistency *can* emerge from particular emotional states, and he considers the altruistic emotions to be an adequate foundation for moral action. However, it would be difficult to demonstrate that altruistic emotions are constant and consistently present throughout humanity. This is not uncontroversial, and we shall see in the next chapter that there are competing views on whether there is a universal altruistic sentiment. One way of redeeming the foundational role Blum gives to the emotions is (along evolutionary lines) to construe them as powerful instincts that 'pull' us towards certain actions. However, as we shall discover, there is nothing especially moral, or indeed altruistic, about our instincts. Although emotions (as instincts) can clearly be responsive – one can have a response that is to need and act on such a response – the additional stipulation that those responses be altruistic cannot be guaranteed. Further, Blum assigns a sophisticated cognitive role to the altruistic emotions through their capacity to recognize others as needy and to assess the nature of their needs, and it is hard to square these more reason-based roles with the interpretation of emotions as instincts.

Plainly, arriving at a morally defensible yet psychologically realistic account of altruism and motivation is no simple task. Where the Kantian framework gives us a rigid, reliable structure, it fails to recognize our everyday experience of altruism which has a significant emotional input. However, where emotions do have a constitutive role in the definition of altruism, they do not give us the confidence we can gain from moral principles which stand independent of our individual malleable natures. However, it may be better to not allow a theoretical conflict to paralyse our action. People act from different motives and display different kinds of altruism in different circumstances, and it seems more important to encourage more action for the sake of others than worry about the best theoretical category in which to place it. This is not to say that *post facto* assessment and evaluation of altruism is not important. But if some people's altruism is more rational and others' more sentimental in nature then we can each be critics of others' endeavours. In the next chapter we shall explore evolutionary ideas that attempt to explain how we came to be the kinds of beings that have a deep concern for the welfare of others; and in Chapter 4 we shall consider some examples of altruistic behaviour, some of it more principled, some more emotive in nature. Before doing so, however, we shall, in the remainder of this chapter, further interrogate the relationship between altruism and morality by considering three more areas where they inter-sect: supererogation, reciprocity and (im)partiality.

Supererogation

Supererogatory acts are those beyond the call of duty or beyond what is morally required of us; actions which go the extra mile and are praiseworthy on just that account. Unlike our moral duties, most philosophers consider us not blameworthy if we fail to engage in supererogatory acts. Kant consider altruism (interpreted as beneficence) to be supererogatory in just this sense. However, on the face of it this would imply that we have no duty to be altruistic and hence it is not something we ought to strive to be. If, on the contrary, we do consider at least some kinds of altruism to come within the purview of our duties, we need to know just how much, as altruists, we are morally obliged to do. We cannot demand of people that they do things beyond the range of normal skills and abilities, nor that we all should be saints, heroes or such reckless do-gooders that we risk harming ourselves. Not everyone can be a Mother Theresa, not least because this would sacrifice important duties we owe to ourselves to make our lives fulfilling (Wolf 1982). It is reasonable to place fair demands on the extent of the altruistic sacrifice that can be asked of people, even if what they are asked to give up is merely time.

Marcia Baron (1987) distinguishes explicitly between altruistic acts that are obligatory, and those that are permissible and supererogatory. Some instances of altruism are a matter of duty. If I witness a road accident, and I am a qualified first aider, I have a moral obligation to help (Fabre 2004). Even if I am not so qualified, I ought at least to call an ambulance and give such assistance as I can until it arrives. This latter duty is underwritten by good Samaritan laws in some countries where one can be penalized for failing to help. (It is arguable, however, that such penalties mean good Samaritans no longer help from altruistic motives (Seglow 2004).) If in this accident, a fire is started in the car and the driver is trapped, rescuing them would involve me in considerable risk to myself, illustrating that it is not merely the good one can do, but also the risks one incurs that determines whether an act is supererogatory or morally obligatory. Finally, as we have seen, there are things that are generally good to do, but which we are under no moral obligation to do. It's great when my neighbour helps me load the van when I'm moving house, but it would be a bit extreme to insist that he has a moral obligation to do so. Some philosophers, however, would not let us off the hook so easily. We could classify commonplace altruism of the helping kind not as a matter of supererogation but as a question of imperfect duties. The latter are duties where we are blameworthy if we fail to fulfil them, but where agents have choice and discretion in where to direct their energies. My neighbour might have an aversion to heavy lifting, but if he gives some free time to helping children to read in our local primary school, he has met his imperfect altruistic duty.

One very common way many of us are altruistic is in donating money to charity, although whether this is supererogatory, imperfect or obligatory, is a matter of debate. Peter Singer (1972) famously argued from a negative utilitarian position – where we have a strong duty to alleviate suffering as far as we can – that our duties to famine victims in the third world are stringent and extensive. As a utilitarian, Singer asks us to consider what benefits we would give up in order to bring help to others. The general principle he advances is this: 'if it is in our power to prevent something bad from happening, without thereby sacrificing anything of comparable moral importance, we ought morally to do it' (Singer 1972: 231). Since the luxuries which make our lives that much more pleasant hardly compare in significance to the gift of life, we do have a strong duty to alleviate famine and abject poverty. In contrast to the way many givers consider their charitable endeavours, Singer would not consider their action altruistic just on account of it being a strong duty. However, this raises the question of whether there is a space between duties of justice and situations where we have no real obligation to help because people's need is not urgent. If there is no such space, it is hard to see what work the category of altruism applied to charity could do. We shall return to this in Chapter 5 when we consider the role of altruism in the welfare state.

Reciprocity

The notion of reciprocity is firmly embedded in the common moral consciousness as complaints about welfare 'scroungers' and unemployed 'layabouts' loudly testify. Like altruism, the idea of reciprocity is based on a fundamental recognition of human beings as social creatures, able to give and to receive benefits. However, while altruism urges us to benefit others, at least when we are responding to their needs, the idea of reciprocity reminds us that, as not everyone is enough of an altruist, those who are at risk of being exploited by the others if their giving is not returned. Thus reflection on justice, equality and fairness of treatment, enjoins us to examine reciprocity as we consider altruism. Max Scheler (whom we encountered in Chapter 1) argued that altruism does not comprehend the idea of reciprocity, and certainly the thoroughgoing unconditional altruist seems a character ripe for exploitation by others. Perhaps altruism is after all a blinkered, irrational commitment in a world of actors who would quite readily take advantage of someone's charity to benefit themselves? Perhaps altruists do not properly attend to their own needs and interests? Nietzsche held this view, treating altruism as an unacceptable martyrdom, where a person enslaved themselves to the needs of others and in the process destroyed themselves. Certainly, the optimistic view that every person could be so focused on the concerns and needs of others that no one need be concerned about their own welfare seems far-fetched, indeed utopian.

The notion of reciprocity seeks to address this problem, while maintaining a commitment to the selfless act. The Golden Rule (treat others as you would have them treat you) is perhaps best read as a principle of reciprocity in that it stresses the mutuality of our obligations. Kant's principle of beneficence, although placing the responsibility and initiative to act beneficently to another at the feet of the individual agent, also depends on a process that uses reciprocation as its rationale. Kant argues that one has a duty to be beneficent, because it would be irrational to forgo the possible help one might need from others in the future. Thus in place of utopian altruism, we can imagine a scenario of mutual recognition of human needs and exchanges of aid in a social context where all acknowledge their duties. This is something that Barbara Herman has identified in Kant as the duty of mutual aid (Herman 1993).

Reciprocity provides a way of protecting the altruist by emphasizing the value of exchange. However, it is far from clear whether the reciprocators have the same kinds of praiseworthy motivations that pure altruists do. Am I motivated to benefit someone, *because* of what I might get in return? If so, I could hardly claim to be an altruist (after all, such exchanges characterize most market transactions). We can distinguish here between reciprocity that depends on conditions of reasonable exchange, and reciprocity that is by contrast incidental to the giving act. In the first case, a company might, for example, agree to giving money to a charity as long as the charity puts the company's logo on all its future promotions as 'free' advertising. Without the logo appearing, the money would not be forthcoming, casting doubt on the altruistic motivations of company executives. With the second kind of reciprocity, it would seem to be only fair that if a person has benefited from another's selfless act of giving, they ought to do something in return, regardless of whether it is expected of them.

For example, one of us (Niall Scott) has an informal arrangement with a disabled colleague. I give him a lift to work when he happens to be going in at the same time as I am. We have had a discussion about sharing petrol money, but as I would have been driving in anyway it seems unfair to ask for this. Instead, my colleague buys me breakfast. Sometimes I do not give him a ride, but he buys me breakfast anyway; at other times I do give him a ride, but he does not buy breakfast – one of us may have an early meeting or lecture. In this arrangement, reciprocity is not presumed but it is made available. The offer of a lift is unconditional, it still stands even if I receive nothing in return. In this sense the exchange (breakfast) is incidental to my giving, however welcome it is. Further (unlike a case where we divide the petrol money), there is no calculation by either side of the return gift being worth a comparable amount to the original gift. Altruists can accept reciprocation even if they do not demand it.

The first view of reciprocity, where each side avoids exploitation by others through insisting that what they are given is of comparable worth, faces the problem that it is not always possible to exchange an eye for an eye. Some people (the old, the infirm or those already saddled with significant responsibilities to others) may simply be unable to give something of comparable value to what they receive. But neither is it reasonable to insist that they do so. As Richard Arneson argues, 'someone who confers slight benefit on me at huge cost to himself does not plausibly trigger an obligation on my part to pay him back a comparable benefit at comparable huge cost' (Arneson 1997: 16). It is debatable whether there is anything intrinsic to the idea of reciprocity that returns must be comparable but, having said that, a market-led as opposed to a more altruistic social ethos may encourage reciprocators to be on the lookout for comparable exchanges. What is more certain is that if social relationships are shaped by felt obligations to return 'favours' or similar feelings of indebtedness to the giver, the commendable voluntary nature of altruistic giving is seriously damaged. I may repay you a favour, because I feel bound by your kindness beyond mere gratitude. But if I become motivated by the urge to release myself from debt, not by kindness, I start to build my actions on different reasons, different motivations. Reciprocation, if it is to remain truly altruistic, needs to avoid the encroaching egoism that can muddy the motivational waters where equal treatment is expected, or a recipient is held to an obligation rather than being free to make an independent decision about giving back in return.

Partiality and impartiality

The topic of (im)partiality brings together moral and political philosophy, combining as it does ideas of equal treatment with demands of justice. It raises some difficult issues for altruists, especially those motivated by compassionate or empathetic responses to particular situations or those who have good reasons to favour particular others (such as family members) over the impartial welfare of all. Before considering this, let us first look at impartiality in more detail.

The impartial point of view has its source in the principle that everybody counts and in the ideal of equal human worth. Reasoning impartially requires agents to detach themselves from their own projects and preferences and to consider the situation at hand from a disinterested, impersonal point of view. This does not mean that everybody involved in the situation must be treated equally. It's important to distinguish between being treated as an equal and receiving equal treatment (Dworkin 1977: 227). The former is a requirement of impartiality, the latter need not be. For example, in an accident with multiple casualties, a choice may have to be made as to whom one should rescue first. In such a case it is practically impossible for all to receive equal treatment. Indeed, for prudential reasons, it may make sense to rescue those least injured first, in order that they might help provide assistance in rescuing others. Provided we have good reasons for whatever system of priority we adopt, each person is still treated as an equal.

Sometimes it's said that impartiality implies a God's eye point of view, and it's certainly true that I need to be able to step outside my own skin as an impartialist. I must consider myself as simply one among others. Kant's and more recently Nagel's (1991) moral theories are impartialist ones; both of them enjoin us to treat ourselves as any other and assess what ought to be done

when each person's interests count equally. Both are deontologi-
cal theories where there are universally applicable principles that
apply to the moral treatment of all other agents, and individuals
are rationally committed to the universal point of view merely by
dint of being moral reasoners. The version of Kant's categorical
imperative which holds that we ought never to treat another
human being merely as a means to our own ends, is an example of
this kind of impartial moral reasoning. Consequentialist impartialists, by contrast, while also starting from the axiom that each
person's interests count equally, see those interests as goals to be
promoted. Impartiality is manifested in the fact that some people's (my own or others') private interests may have to be
sacrificed in order to maximize interest-satisfaction overall.
Peter Singer's argument that citizens of rich countries have a duty
to alleviate the suffering of the global poor, since we can do so
without enduring any comparable suffering ourselves, is an example of impartialist consequentialist reasoning. (Singer's argument
is actually a negative consequentialist one since we are obliged
only to minimize suffering, not to maximize well-being.) Singer
is adamant that geographical proximity and other forms of relatedness have no bearing on the strength of this obligation. 'The
fact that a person is physically near to us, so that we have personal
contact with him, may make it more likely that we *shall* assist
him, but this does not show that we ought to help him rather than
another who happens to be further away' (Singer 1972: 232). A
further way of construing impartiality is through the notion of an
'ideal observer' – someone who is capable of considering a
situation infallibly absent of any bias or other failure of moral
reasoning. However, achieving such a status is quite a challenge,
and the theory is open to the criticism that ideal observers are too
distant from actual situations to have a proper understanding of
the lives of those human beings involved (Jollymore 2006).

Altruists live closer to the ground. There is so much good that
can be done in the world, and altruists are prepared to make
sacrifices to do some – often those they are most familiar with.
Thus an important constituent of altruism, at least on some
interpretations of the idea, is the element of discretion. Altruists
are praiseworthy on account of the good that they did, and not
blameworthy for not doing other good things. Sometimes this is a
matter of conscious choice, sometimes not. I might make a
rational decision to support a certain charity, but may also be

moved by my compassionate feelings towards helping the beggar who stands in front of me. Impartialists and altruists will agree that we should (often at least) promote others' interests, not our self-interest, and that it is better to do some good than none at all. However, where a person chooses to aid their family, friends, neighbours or compatriots over strangers whose needs may be greater, impartialists will become suspicious. Even if we feel *compelled* to help our nearest and dearest, that does not mean we cannot educate ourselves to expand the range of our moral sympathies. After all, impartialists tend to say, motivation is one thing but justification quite another.

One way out of this dilemma is to connect impartiality and altruism conceptually through the idea that the impersonal point of view is a necessary feature of altruistically motivated actions. This is Nagel's (1970) strategy. On the impersonal perspective one is simply a person among others, where descriptions from this 'standpoint do not require the first person or other token reflexives' (Nagel 1970: 101). Thus, what is held to be true concerning oneself can be held to be true of any other person. The personal perspective, on the other hand, views the world from a particular standpoint within it. Altruism does not belong there. This seems counter-intuitive, however, and (as we explored above) may rid the altruist of motivational resources.

Another strategy is the distinction made by Brian Barry (1995) among others between first-order and second-order moral principles. The idea is that impartiality only applies at the second-order, there is no requirement that people exhibit first-order impartiality. First-order *partiality* involves the ordinary, perhaps mundane, range of choices that occur regularly in human existence. It is perfectly acceptable that some of our daily decisions will be partial. Indeed, when we think, for example, of parents' preference for looking after their own children, it is hard to understand how they could not be. Thus first-order impartiality gives agents some room to promote their own interests, as well as those of others they are close to. This behaviour, however, operates within a framework defined by second-order impartiality. The latter involves principles of justice and institutional rules which embody them. Thus individuals are free philanthropically to give away their private resources (or alternatively to hoard them), but through the adoption of principles of social justice embodied in the tax-welfare system some of those they may choose to help are assisted anyway by the state.

The first/second-order distinction seems to fit nicely the distinction between perfect and imperfect duties, at least as regards some of the latter. Looking after one's own children, admittedly, is a perfect duty, but many areas of the private, personal realm are the province of imperfect duties (Kant's duty of beneficence, for example); perfect duties, by contrast, are those institutionalized in law and subject to coercive authority. Does this mean that we can happily be first-order but not second-order altruists? Perhaps not. Moral distinctions are not always matched by psychological ones, and people may resent the coercive imposition of second-order requirements and wish to be altruists through and through, at every level. Conversely, if impartiality is stressed, can we still be genuine altruists? As Jurgen De Wispelaere asks 'if the altruist is motivated by impartiality does this not render altruistic dispositions obsolete?' (De Wispelaere 2004: 23). We shall return to these questions when we consider altruism and justice in Chapter 5.

3

Altruism and evolution

We have looked at what motivates us to be altruistic and how such motivation is possible, but this does not explain how something like altruism as a form of behaviour could have come about. In Chapter 1, we looked at the history of altruism in philosophy and considered briefly how evolutionary theory contributed to that history. In this chapter, we will look at a different kind of historical question: how could altruistic behaviour have evolved? What explains it? We shall see that the terms 'altruism' and 'egoism' take on quite a different meaning in an evolutionary vocabulary than they do in the language of ethics. However, there is still a relationship between the evolutionary conception of altruism and the moral one, as we shall see. In the discussion of altruism and evolution, many disciplines come together: evolutionary biology, philosophy, psychology, game theory and the broad discipline of evolutionary ethics and sociobiology to name but a few, and it is quite a challenge to follow the impact of the discussion through all these areas. Nevertheless, this is what we shall seek to do.

To start out, let us try to define altruism in evolutionary terms. This definition will be unpacked in more detail as this chapter progresses. In the context of evolution, altruism is self-sacrificial behaviour that results in an increase in the chances of an individual's genes being represented in the next generation. Thus as Eliot Sober puts it, '[e]volutionary altruism has to do with the reproductive consequences of behaviour' (Sober 1998: 462). Evolutionary altruism does not, on this definition, concern itself with the motivations or other psychological mechanisms that are involved in such behaviour, which were our interest earlier. Sober additionally claims that since this definition is about reproductive consequences, and not motives, it can be applied to every kind of organism, not just to human beings. The evolutionary perspective on altruism is not especially interested in morality *per se*, which is regarded as a social artifice. Indeed, evolutionary biologists tend to explain our propensity to act in ways which benefit others in terms of genetics rather than broader ideas of culture or society.

Sober usefully distinguishes between evolutionary and vernacular altruism, the latter referring to how the idea is used in an everyday sense. '[V]ernacular altruism is essentially psychological, not essentially reproductive and not essentially comparative. Evolutionary altruism is the opposite' (Sober 1998: 462). Vernacular altruism is the everyday kind of altruism that is associated with human behaviour, and in particular the motivations and dispositions involved in human agency. It is this kind of altruism we think there should be more of in society. It is also referred to by biologists as psychological altruism (Sober and Wilson 1998), literal altruism (Ruse 1990) or human altruism. Evolutionary altruism, by contrast, is not restricted to human behaviour. As Sober puts it:

> [e]volutionary altruism can occur in organisms that don't have minds; and evolutionary altruism involves the donation of reproductive benefits. Evolutionary altruism has to do with the reproductive consequences of behaviour, not with the proximate mechanisms (psychological or otherwise) that guides that behaviour.
>
> (Sober 1998: 462)

In recent years, much attention has been devoted to explaining evolutionary perspectives on selfish and unselfish behaviour in countless books that popularize the philosophy of biology and evolutionary theory. The main debate surrounding the issue of altruism concerns whether or not there is room for truly unselfish behaviour in evolutionary theory, especially the kind of (vernacular) altruism that is required for moral behaviour. As Janet Radcliffe-Richards points out: '[m]oral behaviour, whatever its details, must involve the capacity to subject your own interests for the good of others, or to the requirements of moral principles of other kinds' (Radcliffe-Richards 2000: 154). The very idea of comparing one's own and others' interests, and deciding that, sometimes at least, the former should yield to the latter, presupposes a notion of moral agency that is simply absent from the evolutionary perspective on animal behaviour.

Indeed, as some evolutionary biologists believe that animals (humans and others) naturally seek to promote only their own interests, they have great difficulty in explaining how altruism occurs. Preyed upon by their more selfish fellows, altruists ought to die out quite quickly. However, many solutions to this core problem have been proposed, all seeking to show how altruism can persist, indeed flourish. For example, Sober (1998) argues that evolutionary altruism is essentially comparative. By this he means that, although, in terms of individual's reproductive success, it tends to be better to be selfish than selfless; a group of altruists provide benefits for each other and, hence, if one does live in a group of altruists it is better to be altruistic. This is a key part of the evolutionary explanation of how altruism persists in a world of beings selfishly concerned only with their reproductive success, as we shall see.

The relationship between biology and morality has a substantial history, the work of Lamarck or Auguste Comte (who championed a science of the brain), for example, stand out. But questions about if and how one could inherit a moral tendency or moral sense were most clearly articulated by Charles Darwin in *The Descent of Man* (1871). Darwin argued that one could explain altruism in terms of group selection. While an altruistic individual might suffer on account of their altruism, their group might benefit and, hence, even if the individual perished, the group would, on account of some of its members' altruism, survive and persist. Put another way, altruism, for Darwin, could be explained in terms of the fitness of the group, which was enhanced at the cost an individual's prospects for survival (Rosenberg 1998). (The term 'fitness' is a measure of the ability of a population to survive the process of natural selection. It is a ratio of the number of individuals produced in relation to the number of individuals needed to keep that population at a constant size.)

In the development of unselfish behaviour, sympathy was the key for Darwin. The evolution of sympathy and related behaviours that were directed towards others in the same community were, according to Darwin, beneficial for survival, starting with the benefits conferred by social living: 'With those animals which were benefited by living in close association, the individuals which took the greatest pleasure in society would best escape various dangers; whilst those that cared least for their comrades and lived solitarily would perish in greater numbers' (Darwin 1874: 102). Darwin identifed sympathy as having especial value because of its function utility in social groups:

> in however a complex manner this feeling may have originated, as it is one of high importance to all those animals which aid and defend one another, it will have increased through natural selection; for those communities, which included the greatest number of the most sympathetic members, would flourish best, and rear the greatest number of offspring.
>
> (Darwin 1871: 103)

For Darwin sympathy was the origin of the human moral sense. (His ideas seem to owe something to those of the British empiricist moralists, such as Shaftesbury, Hutcheson and Hume.) However, sympathy, like all our characteristic feelings and forms of behaviour, has a complex causal history. It was not clear, Darwin writes, which of our behaviours 'were acquired through natural selection or are the indirect result of other instincts and faculties such as sympathy, reason, experience and a tendency to imitation, or again whether they are simply the result of long continued habit' (Darwin 1874: 103–4).

Darwin's explanation for the persistence of altruism hinges on his idea that natural selection occurs in groups, not merely in individuals. Alleles (sets of genes in one locus, such as a species), will continue to be passed down successive generations of a group because of the advantages they bring to it. Altruistic behaviour by some of its members, in part genetically determined, will benefit the group through improving its evolutionary fitness, even if, at the same time, the altruistic individuals will in all likelihood sacrifice their reproductive interests in favour of the group. This theory was originally articulated in terms of altruism by V. C. Wynne-Edwards in 1962. An ecologist and ornithologist, he developed the idea of group selection based on his observation of breeding behaviours and population structures in birds, and mainly on his studies of grouse. Wynne-Edwards observed that grouse sometimes failed to reproduce when their flock was threatened with a shortage of food. He suggested that large collections of animals, such as flocks of birds, are able to assess their size in relation to their food supply and forgo reproduction in a way that ensures the survival of the group (Wynne-Edwards 1962).

The theory of group selection, however, has been vigorously criticized, the main criticism being that a group of altruists may easily be undermined by selfish individuals in their group, who, taking advantage of the giving, sharing and self-sacrificing behaviour of the altruists, will flourish at their expense. Thus Matt Ridley (1997) questions what happens when what is good for the group (or species) is bad for the individual. According to game theory (to be explored below), it is only individuals who have interests, not hypostatic entities like groups. There are no functional prerequisites of group survival which can direct individual behaviour. Ridley confidently asserts that: 'biologists have thoroughly undermined the whole logic of group selection. It is now an edifice without foundation' (Ridley 1997: 175). Along similar lines John Maynard Smith (1988) refers to group selection as a Panglossian fallacy, referring to Voltaire's character Dr Pangloss (a satire on Leibnitz) in his novel *Candide* who thought that everything was for the best in the best of all possible worlds. Maynard Smith sees no special reason to support the idea that group selection allows the best possible adaptations to occur for the benefit of the group. There are just as likely to be adaptations with maleficent consequences for the group. However, it is not certain that altruism requires the best possible adaptations, even if it does require that most adaptations are not maleficent.

Sociobiology

As we mentioned, sociobiology is another discipline that shares an interest in altruism and evolution, indeed it is one of the more important disciplines. The term 'sociobiology' was coined in 1975 by E. O. Wilson in his book, *Sociobiology: The New Synthesis*. The discipline investigates the nature of the different kinds of relationships that exist between organisms. In particular, it seeks to understand the connection between social behaviour and the results of evolution, and indeed to substantiate the claim that there is an important connection between the two. As Daniel Dennet has noted, sociobiology has probably been responsible for some of the most important recent contributions to theoretical biology (Dennet 1995). Sociobiologists have been greatly interested by evolutionary explanations of the phenomena of altruistic and egoistic behaviour. However, sociobiologists are often too quick in inferring conclusions about the moral behaviour of human beings simply from their genetic adaptations: their arguments which bridge this gap are often quite poor. They tend to blur the boundary between the strict evolutionary definition of altruism given above and moral – or vernacular – definitions.

For one thing, this jumps what moral philosophers have called the is/ought gap. Evolution is simply a process. We may be entitled to draw some conclusions from it about how humans (and other animals) have behaved, morally or otherwise, but we cannot ground moral values concerning how we ought to behave in a set of merely evolutionary facts. For another, as Stephen Jay Gould has pointed out, the relationship between genetic adaptation and behaviour is far more complex in humans than it is in other animals because of the way that social and cultural factors explain so much human behaviour (Gould 1980). To be fair, some sociobiologists recognize these problems and draw back from simple genetics to behavioural inferences. But instead of dismissing sociobiology entirely because of these difficulties, it is better to see the questions it poses as part of challenge of evolutionary ethics. If it is worth trying to theorize the relationship between the content of morality, as moral philosophers understand it, and evolutionary (including sociobiological) explanations for the origins of morality, because such a theory would have enormous explanatory power and normative purchase. Moral philosophers would only suggest we ought to do what we are evolutionarily capable of doing; and conversely sociobiologists would only try to account for how we actually should seek to behave.

Kin altruism

As we have seen, a key question that besets evolutionary theorists and philosophers of biology is whether altruism is possible at all, given that an individual's selfish behaviour is more likely to be evolutionarily successful than their altruistic behaviour. Evolutionary theorists have therefore sought to understand how it might be possible to gain an evolutionary competitive advantage through altruistic behaviour. This is a problem when we look at altruism in genetic terms. If genes are the focus of concern, then what matters is an organism's acting in such a way that its genes are present in the next generation. Organisms are programmed so as to maximize the chances of this happening. If altruism involves sacrificial behaviour, such that all the organism's energies go into supporting other organisms rather than its own genes' reproduction, altruistic organisms would quickly die out. However highly we value selfless acts, in humans at least, the evolutionary perspective seems to suggest that those kinds of behaviours would be selected against in the long run, and hence altruism as a trait would not survive. Altruism would simply not be an evolutionarily stable behavioural strategy. On the evolutionary paradigm, altruistic individuals could only flourish if they enjoyed some adaptive benefit as a result of their altruism. Obviously, if altruism is strictly defined as non-beneficial self-sacrifice, then this is impossible. However it is defined, evolutionary theory faces the problem of explaining how the phenomenon of altruism – which is present in insect behaviour through to human behaviour – plainly can persist and yet is incompatible with the general theory of natural selection.

Evolutionary ethics and evolutionary psychology have sought to explain the origins of altruistic and moral behaviour through developing the idea of strategies of co-operation. In humans and other complex mammals, such strategies are sufficiently complex that they constitute a real social and political environment, one in which altruism is a successful adaptive course. There is a complex history to the debate on these ideas, and we shall not enter into the details of it here. At the heart of it is the reduction of explanation to the level of the gene, where what matters is that the organism should behave so as to maximize the chances of its genetic information being passed on to future generations through reproduction.

Co-operative strategy theories begin by distinguishing two planes of explanation: the organism and the gene. If what matters is the passing on of genes, then an organism might forgo reproduction if it can, nonetheless, pass on a proportion of its genes to the next generation through the survival of a relative. (The more closely related organisms are, the greater the proportion of genes shared between them, so ideally the relative would be a close one). Co-operative theories all claim, then, that co-operative behaviour between two kin would be more advantageous for both parties, if related, than competitive behaviour, in terms of genetic survival.

Kin selection is one example of a co-operative strategy theory (we shall consider some others shortly). The term 'kin selection' and the ideas surrounding it was developed by William Hamilton (1964) through his work on hymenoptera (one of the larger orders of insects comprising sawflies, wasps, bees and ants), and is an improvement on the ideas found in group selection theory. Kin selection theory supported the sociobiologists' agenda, and Darwin's thoughts on altruism in insects in *The Descent of Man*. In fact, the idea can again be traced back to a passage in *The Descent of Man*.

> It is evident that with mankind the instinctive impulses have different degrees of strength; a savage will risk his own life to save that of a member of the same community, but will be wholly indifferent about a stranger: a young and timid mother urged by the maternal instinct will, without a moment's hesitation, run the greatest danger for her own infant, but not for a mere fellow-creature.
>
> (Darwin 1871: 87)

A gene is likely to spread in a population if it increases the fitness of an individual. If altruism is looked at as a trait that increases the fitness of others, then it too may increase in frequency in a population rather than die out. By looking at the relationship between cost, benefit and relatedness, Hamilton showed how it was possible for altruism to persist, indeed spread, through natural selection. Cost and benefit are measured in terms of reproductive fitness: a form of behaviour that makes an individual more likely to pass on its genes is a benefit: if it is less likely, it is a cost. Relatedness measures the number of identical genes the altruist shares with the recipient. If there is a close relationship between genes and behaviour, then altruism as a trait will spread through a population when a benefit to others is greater than the cost, but this will depend on the degree of relatedness between the altruist and the beneficiary. The more closely related the altruist is to its beneficiary, the more likely it is that altruism as a trait will be possessed by both.

The upshot of Hamilton's theory is that organisms are more likely to be altruistic towards close relatives than strangers. Not only that, but the more closely related organisms are, the more likely they are to be altruistic. Indeed, an altruistic organism might completely forgo the opportunity to reproduce and instead put all its efforts into ensuring the reproductive success of close family members in which its genes are represented. Hamilton demonstrated that this was true with social insects, such as bees.

It is important to remember that even though the terms 'relatedness' and 'kin' are used here, the process of selection is entirely driven by genetic factors (Ruse 1973: 58). It is the gene that 'wants' to get as many copies of itself as possible into the next generation. Supporting this gene-centred approach is Richard Dawkins' well-known argument that organisms are in essence gene carriers and it is genes that use organisms in order to reproduce themselves rather than the other way around (Dawkins, 1976). Altruism is simply one of genes' means to do this, as is co-operative behaviour more generally. As Michael Ruse has put it, altruism is a collective illusion fobbed off on us by our genes (Ruse 1991: 506).

Some readers may think that this gives genes intentions, which they plainly do not have. Biologists and philosophers of biology defend the language of strategy and intentionality as simply a metaphorical way of talking about genetic reproduction. However, the reductionism of kin selection, sociobiology, and other gene-centred views is not without its critics. Janna Thompson (1982) accuses sociobiology of being an undisciplined collection of theses and models relating the biological and the social rather than being a discipline as such. She notes that when under attack from one angle, say a biological angle, sociobiology can resort to a defence using the social, and vice versa. In particular, she criticizes sociobiology for shifting from a strong claim to a weaker one concerning altruism; the latter is more defensible but is not distinctively sociobiological. Thus when attacked for holding that altruistic behaviour is simply biologically programmed and maintained over time by the preservation of 'altruistic' genes, sociobiologists tend to retreat to a more anodyne view of niceness to others:

> [T]hus we no longer have an urge to be altruistic according to the degree to which other people are biologically related to us, but a more generalized urge to be nice to people who are close to us. Sometimes the urge itself is diluted: it's always there but can be overridden by contingencies.

Usually to be on the safe side, sociobiologists both gener-
alize and dilute these innate inclinations or drives.

(Thompson 1982: 33)

Under pressure, the evolutionary definition of altruism seems
to become a vernacular view, with all the problems of agency,
motive, and their non-biological causes attendant upon it.

Reciprocal altruism

Adherents of kin selection and other theories that seek to explain
how altruism could be evolutionarily successful, have also considered the evolutionary origins of similar types of co-operative
behaviour, such as reciprocity. We earlier discussed how far
reciprocity could be considered a moral ideal; here it is treated
merely as a strategy (not unlike Hobbes's prudential interpretation of the Golden Rule). Evolutionary theorists' analyses of
co-operation and its components have become quite complex
when considered as *strategies*, behavioural patterns an individual
will manifest in order to increase their chances of survival, or
indeed achieve some more mundane goal. Initially used as a tool
to model and predict behaviour in economics, game theory has
been usefully applied to evolutionary behaviour, where it models
and predicts how organisms (plants and animals) respond to other
organisms' behaviour. If reproductive behaviours or behaviours
that have an influence on reproductive strategies can be modelled
and predicted, an insight can be gained into reproductive out-
comes, including whether a trait is likely to persist in a population.

Game theorists have concerned themselves with how far
co-operative and non-co-operative kinds of behaviour can be
predicted through modelling the interactions between organisms
with different sets of assumptions or rules of the game. In
particular, game theory treats the interactions between organisms
as competitions (mirroring the 'survival of the fittest' in natural
selection), where there are winners and losers or, more generally,
'payoffs' for the parties. Game theory was first applied to evolutionary biology by John Maynard Smyth (1988). Evolutionary
approaches to the approach do not require the players to have the
strategic rational capacities distinctive of human beings, such as
the ability to choose, plan and calculate; rather the players, from

non-human species, organisms through to genes have strategies hardwired into them – they cannot act in any other way. The crucial thing is to see which strategies are optimal in maximizing fitness, or which strategies generate stability in a population. Strategies which model the possible behaviours that an organism can engage in are often set out in terms of matrices that set out the comparative payoffs and losses to the players of the game.

The most well-known game in game theory, the prisoner's dilemma, is particularly relevant to altruism. Here the players display strategies of either co-operation (altruistic behaviour) or defection (egoistic behaviour). If both parties co-operate they both gain; if both defect they both lose. However, if one party defects while the other co-operates the former gains while the latter loses even more than if both defected. Since, in the prisoner's dilemma (and indeed in all theoretical games), neither side knows which strategy the other will adopt before they adopt it, both sides have a strong incentive to defect, thereby enjoying a lesser payoff than if they had co-operated. The challenge for the evolutionary biologist committed to the existence of altruism is to show how co-operation is possible given this set up. Fairly complex scenarios and interactions can be modelled as games and iterated (played again and again), with the players learning from their payoff experiences.

Reciprocal altruism, the term coined by Robert Trivers (1971), is altruism that is performed with the hope of obtaining a future reward from the person one benefits. It is not restricted to kin. Game theorists have captured it by modelling the strategic behaviour of individuals where an agent performing an altruistic act only continues to do so if the recipient of their altruism returns the favour. This was called 'tit-for-tat' by Robert Axelrod (1984) and might also be expressed colloquially as 'you scratch my back and I'll scratch yours'. (If reciprocity is moralized with the stipulation that each side *ought* to behave to the other in just that way that they would like the other to behave towards them, then we have the standard version of the Golden Rule – 'do unto others as you would have them do unto you' – but game theory makes no stipulation about the parties' moral sense or lack of it.)

Axelrod modelled the idea of reciprocity in a computer tournament where competing strategies in the prisoners' dilemma game were submitted by various people. The one that dominated the tournament was the strategy submitted by Anatol Rappaport, 'tit-for-tat', under which the player followed the tactic of co-operating on the first move (iteration) of the game and then copied what the other player did in the previous move. Thus if player A co-operated, player B co-operated next time; if A defected, then so too would B (Axelrod 1984). The success of Rappaport's strategy at out-competing the others' submissions to the tournament lay in the fact that those who did not reciprocate favours were in subsequent rounds ignored, so unco-operative behaviour was punished, and co-operators would do well as long as reciprocity continued between them. Given certain minimal assumptions about players' ability to learn from their experience – but no assumption that co-operation is morally the better thing to do – Axelrod found that tit-for-tat led to an equilibrium of perpetual mutual co-operation as it produced the greatest payoffs for both parties when the prisoners' dilemma was iterated again and again. The significance of this result is that it shows how altruism can emerge as a stable result even when, as in the amoral world of the struggle for survival, no side regards it as a superior way to behave.

Tit-for-tat was, nonetheless, criticized for not demonstrating genuine altruism, since it merely involves an exchange of favours (or disfavours); an act is performed on the assumption that it will be repaid. In one sense, of course, this is quite right. Game theoretic agents are not interested in benefiting the other for the other's sake. But we must be careful to attend to our distinction between evolutionary and vernacular altruism. Reciprocity may seldom be altruistic in a vernacular sense, but in the morally deracinated world of natural selection altruistic behaviour, defined by its consequences not the intentions behind it, just *is* the more co-operative strategy.

After the original game theory competition, subsequent tournaments included more complex kinds of games, that attempted to model multiple variables in animal environments. One example is the ecological tournament (Axelrod 1986). Here, the points scored by programs in previous tournaments were interpreted as a measure of fitness, interpreted in turn as the number of offspring organisms would produce in the next generation. From an equal representation of programs (organisms) at the beginning, the environment changes as programs are defeated (become extinct) or succeed (survive). In these cases of iterated tournaments, tit-for-tat was again successful, Axelrod noted, not by defeating its opponents but by rewarding their attempts at co-operation. So in a tournament setup where extinction and survival is being modelled, co-operative behaviour still succeeds, supporting the idea that, though hardly instances of pure altruism, reciprocal and co-operative behaviours can at least evolve to a stable level and maintain themselves in a population.

Other models have been developed that are able to improve on tit-for-tat, such as that introduced by Philip Kitcher in games that involved so-called 'discriminating altruists' (Kitcher 1993). In focusing on the question of how human altruism might have evolved, Kitcher's version considers the case of 'cognitively sophisticated organisms' who are not locked into the game but can choose to play, or not to play, against each other – or choose to play with some but not others. Prior to the game, players can identify the types of opponent they may have to face and employ discriminating strategies in deciding whether to play them or not. According to Kitcher:

> Discriminating Altruists (DAs) are prepared to play with any organism that has never willingly defected on them and when they play, always co-operate, Willing defectors (WDs), are always prepared to play and always defect. Solos (Sos) always opt out. Selective defectors (SDs) are prepared to play with any organism that has never defected on them and always defect.
>
> (Kitcher 1993: 501)

The aim of this tournament was to show that co-operating behaviour could evolve and persist despite the emphasis on egoism in the theory of natural selection. The model suggest that it pays to co-operate.

The study of the evolution of co-operation, in terms of modelling, reflects a continuing preoccupation on the part of game theorists with trying to understand the relationship between evolutionary altruism and the development of *moral* behaviour in human beings. Axelrod, for example, attempted to introduce punishment as a strategy agents could adopt in game tournaments to enforce and reinforce other players' co-operative behaviour. He complicated the game further by also introducing 'meta-norms' where those that failed to punish unco-operative behaviour were in turn subject to punishment (Axelrod 1986). Other games have introduced the idea of players gaining reputations for themselves (as strict punishers or co-operative altruists, for example) so that their behaviour can be recognized and responded to by others with a reasonable degree of accuracy. The idea behind these innovations was to understand how co-operation could be maintained in a population through their adherence to certain 'rules'. Players who adhered to rules which promoted the group's flourishing (modelling evolutionary success) were, by Axelrod's definition, altruistic, but not every player always did because, as is always the case with game theory, each player also had individual interests they sought to promote.

In introducing punishment and other norms, game theory makes a crucial move: it now seeks not merely to describe how co-operation could have come about, but to understand how normative values could have evolved in the highly complex social arena of human behaviour, and indeed to prescribe that we act in certain ways (Dugatkin 2002). Of course, punishment and reward are, as we might put it, proto-moral: to avoid an act just because one knows one will be punished for it is not to recognize that the act is wrong. But proto-morality can evolve into full-blooded morality as agents reflect on why they are liable to punishment (as we shall see in the next chapter, this is how the adult moral sensibility evolves in children). But the problem for game theory is that players with sufficiently advanced cognitive capacities to pursue reward-gaining and punishment-avoiding strategies, and to punish and reward each other, seem now to be intentional agents with their own desires, wishes and goals. And intentional agents are not only extremely difficult for computers to model (computer programs do not have intentions), they are also beyond the explanatory framework of evolutionary altruism, key to which is the notion that individuals are *driven*, by the struggle for survival, to engage in co-operative or competitive forms of behaviour.

The basic question, then, is whether game theory does very much to explain altruism. If reciprocal and co-operative behaviour are really an attempt at securing copies of the altruist's genes and increasing the chances that those genes will be replicated and represented in future generations, then we have only explained altruism in the restricted evolutionary (consequentialist) sense. To explain altruism in the more full-blooded (vernacular) sense, we need to impute more complex features to game theoretic agents, but it is not at all clear that these can be adequately modelled. Game theories have limited explanatory power when dealing with organisms that have extremely complex interactions in large groups, in the way that humans distinctively do.

Green beard altruism

Above we encountered the suggestion that altruism, if it evolves as a trait, is more likely to do so in groups where members are closely related. However, there is a further question as to whether altruism exists as a behaviour between strangers – organisms that are not related. Green beard altruism attempts to deal with the problem of how altruism could have evolved in non-kin (stranger) relationships. It is based on the idea that altruistic individuals may have developed recognizable (phenotypic) characteristics that single them out as altruists – such as sporting a green beard. In reciprocal altruism, a behaviour can be strategically altered in order to respond to another, described above through 'tit-for-tat' strategies. Green beard altruism suggests that altruists may have recognizable traits so that they can associate together and avoid defectors. Those who co-operate recognize one another and those who defect can be excluded, and will eventually die out. It follows, then, that a self-interested individual would do best to co-operate with green beard altruists to avoid the punishment consequent on defecting. Eventually only altruists benefit, since altruists will not respond to individuals without green beards (Fehr and Fischbacher 2005: 73–84).

This idea hinges on the coalescence of several traits associated with one gene: an individual would need to have the trait for altruism, the trait to generate a characteristic heritable tag (a 'green beard') and the capacity for recognizing those tags in others. This may be quite a bit to ask (Jansen and van Baalen 2006). In addition to highly developed memories and cognitive capacities, green beard altruists would also need to be able to make fairly sophisticated inferences about others from their behaviour, and this may not be possible unless there was a necessary relationship between a tag and altruistic behaviour in an organism. Fehr and Fischbacher think that it is unlikely to be possible to distinguish altruistic from non-altruistic human beings perfectly, based only on conspicuous, observable characteristics (Fehr and Fischbacher 2005: 73–84). They point out that, in humans, lying, for example, is not easy to detect. The green beard argument also falters when it assumes that there are no cheaters – individuals who are selfish but have a green beard mutation. These would infiltrate and easily exploit green beard altruists, gaining all the rewards at no cost to themselves. However, according to Frank, such objections can be dealt with by arguing that the theoretical and empirical work done by Fehr and Fischerbacher concern *brief* interactions between protagonists (Frank 2005).

The ability to predict others' altruism reliably is a complex one since it involves developing signals that go beyond the mere mimicry of others' traits. Growing a green beard as a signal to show that you are an altruist, or tend to associate with altruists, is unlikely to be the only signal. Many kinds of complex behaviours and capacities are needed to be able to identify altruists, for example, trust. If human beings do have the ability to recognize other altruists, it would have taken a long time to evolve. Frank argues that such predictive abilities would only have come about after emotions and other behaviours were selected for by evolution. He states:

> The complex and multi-dimensional links between specific emotions and facial expressions, eye movements, the pitch and timbre of the voice, body language and a host of other observable details were well entrenched long before those observable markers could have begun to function as strategic signals.
>
> (Frank 2005: 93)

As such, any development that allows an individual to mimic green beard signalling will also take time to develop, leaving a counter-response or coping time. An organism will need to develop the ability to recognize, remember and trust the green bearded altruist, and adapt to the form of signalling over time – this could not occur instantaneously. As a result, Frank holds that signals of emotions – complex signals – could be very difficult to mimic compared to simple ones.

Frank's arguments usefully remind us of the complexity of altruistic behaviours. The gene-centred view has some explanatory power and may be convincing for simple interactions, such as those in game theory, but it runs into problems with altruism as a sophisticated social behaviour. Notwithstanding the gene-centred explanation of evolutionary altruism, the challenge remains to explain how the phenomenon of altruism could have arisen and become what it is, a *moral* phenomenon. We now turn to consider whether what we have learnt about altruism as an evolutionary strategy might help inform our understanding of altruism as a part of morality.

Bridging the gap between evolutionary and moral altruism

As we suggested, the language of punishment and reward that the more sophisticated game theory seeks to model is proto-moral, and it raises the question of whether full-blooded morality could have evolved from the institutions of punishment and reward. The evolutionary theorist, T. H. Huxley (1898), saw punishment and reward as crucial mechanisms if any animals were to develop a society. If they did, then punishment, reward and responses to them would be institutionalized as tacit rules, the existence of which is constitutive of societies. In his Romanes lectures, Huxley suggested that, in humans, such institutionalization has come to be known as justice. As human beings, we punish and reward each other according to what we believe others deserve, and desert, Huxley plausibly held, involves recognition of others' motives. This is important because acting from the right motive gives us the possible beginnings of a genuinely moral stance (in a way that the mere infliction of punishments and rewards does not). Huxley's speculations suggest how it may have been possible for altruism as a reproductive mechanism to transform itself into a codifiable behaviour.

Huxley saw human moral development as combating the processes of natural selection and the survival of the best adapted fit, so that, as he put it, ethical progress runs counter to cosmic progress (Huxley 1898). Goodness or virtue, in his view, directly opposed just that which the evolutionary approach thought led to most success: ruthless self-assertion. More recently, other morally astute theorists have offered their own accounts of the evolutionary origins of morality. The anthropologist, Christopher Boehm (2000), for example, emphasizes power and the suppression of conflict as proto-moral behaviours, rather than punishment and desert, in an account that is more political than sociological. Boehm reminds us that morality could not have arisen from *ad hoc* responses to deviance, but rather involves a group's collective normative acknowledgement of which behaviours are acceptable and which are not. Game theorists can show how certain strategies are successful, but we need a better account than they are able to offer of how these are sedimented as norms in the moral culture of a group. The anthropological perspective which considers the broader conditions and contexts in which human interactions may have taken place is therefore a useful corrective.

Anthropologists argue that altruistic and other 'pro-social' kinds of behaviour become embedded in a complex range of social relationships that functionally support the political and economic needs of the group. They cannot, contra game theory, be explained as individuals' strategies. For Boehm, the origins of human morality are to be found in the codification of behaviours that deal with conflict and its suppression. Deviance, harm to other group members, and their predatory exploitation are all dysfunctional activities in a group, and are thus subject to the pressure of social control through political coalition forming. He treats the simple banding together of organisms as the rudimentary features of political interaction. Furthermore, groups as moral entities are also constituted by agreement not just on what counts as acceptable behaviour, but also by a teleological conception of a *desirable* social and political life (Boehm 2000: 80).

The emphasis on the political roots of moral behaviour leads Boehm to suggest that resentment at the domination they experience by strong individuals, such as alpha males, could lead those dominated to rebel. The possibility of such a rebellion, and in particular the threat it poses for both sides, is the foundation of a rudimentary egalitarianism. Thus, for example, dominant individuals who seek to maximize their own food consumption put the rest of the early societies under economic pressure, and therefore need to be constrained. This emphasis on coercion sounds quite Hobbesian. If it were, Boehm could not claim to have offered an explanation for morality's origins, for Hobbes's position is that the authoritative source of social norms lies merely in their ability to promote peace; they lack any further normative content. However, in contrast to Hobbes and despite the apparent Hobbesianism of his rebellion thesis, Boehm has a developed notion of group welfare. This is manifested, for example, in the collective response a group may exhibit towards an individual deviant: a preference for dispute resolution over punishment expresses the adoption of a distinctively moral point of view (Boehm 2000: 81).

The view of altruism and morality explicated by Boehm, is beyond the reach of the game theory models of the evolution of altruistic behaviour discussed previously. The kinds of adaptations required for distinctively moral behaviour call for the acquisition of normatively relevant abilities far more complex than the adaptations involved in natural selection as an organ evolves. For example, the normative ideal of non-domination that is involved in a group overcoming their subordination by alpha males requires a cluster of communicative skills, goal-directed reasoning and other complex capacities. Moreover, culture and learning are deeply implicated in moral evolution; this far transcends the way evolving organs better enable specific functions, as the eye, for example, enables us to see (Katz 2000). It is worth noting, however, that, as Boehm ties his account of the emergence of morality to the development of social organization, the nature of that organization is going to shape the morality that emerges. Put simply, Boehm's morality is likely to be socially relative not universal. By contrast, most moral philosophers believe there are fundamental, non-relative moral imperatives that transcend alternative forms of social organization (and hence offer a point of critique upon them), even if at the same time they disagree vehemently over what those imperatives are.

In their significant work, *Unto Others* (1998), Elliot Sober and David Sloan Wilson have similarly attempted to track the relationship between the evolutionary origins of unselfish behaviour and the concept of altruism as a central part of morality. Sober and Wilson stress that theirs is a project of 'descriptive ethics'; they are seeking to explain how our ethical views could have come about, rather than making normative claims about what those views should be. The justification of morality is an altogether different project. Their work is useful, among other reasons, in indicating where the limits of descriptive ethics lie. Further, an important part of their project is to show that dismissals of evolutionary biology's view that altruism could have arisen from group selection are unfounded and, in some cases, fallacious. Sober and Wilson argue, in considerable technical detail, that group selection – where altruists seek out other altruists – is possible, and can thus promote the evolution of altruism, an altruism moreover that is not confined to kin relation-ships. However, they are careful to stress that evolutionary (con-sequentialist) altruism and psychological (vernacular or everyday) altruism are not the same thing and should not be confused. Their interest is carefully directed at what bearing the evolutionary account of altruism has on the psychology of moti-vation. There is, thus, still a gap to be bridged from the descrip-tive to the normative.

Culture, Sober and Wilson suggest, has had an important role in human evolution. Through providing rewards for altruistic behaviour and punishment for selfish behaviour, it has reinforced the prevalence of the former. Co-operative behaviour, thus, could have evolved in part through cultural and social norms which reinforced it, aiding group selection. They admit that the evidence on group selection is much more tentative in humans than it is in non-human species, but claim that there probably has been a similar influence operating among humans (Sober and Wilson 2000). Ultimately, based on this view, the motivation for the emergence of altruistic behaviour was selfish – to avoid punishment and gain reward. Evolutionary altruism, however, is concerned only with the effects of behaviour. The reasons why people began to engage in altruistic behaviour may ultimately have been self-interested ones (and thus not altruistic in a moral sense), but the norms which develop as a result have socially beneficial consequences – and are by that token moral norms. Moreover, though the origins of altruism may involve selfishness, that is not to say that altruism now, as a psychological and moral phenomenon involves selfishness (at least, not all of it). Sober and Wilson do not commit the genetic fallacy of mistaking a thing with its origins. Altruists today do not merely seek to avoid punishment or to gain reward; they desire to satisfy another's needs or wants, or they think that the altruistic action is the right one to do. As we saw in the last chapter, altruistic motivation may best be described as a pluralistic phenomenon.

Sober and Wilson introduce the term 'motivational pluralism' in their description of the evolutionary origins of morality. This, they contend, is the most useful way of describing human interac-tions, and perhaps those of the more sociable animals, and an advance on game theory's tendency to isolate motives as either egoistic or altruistic ones. Motivational pluralism says that we can be motivated by altruistic, egoistic and hedonistic desires; in some activities one of these is more prevalent, in others they all occur together. There are two types of motivational pluralism: one that involves an individual having different motives for different behaviours; the other where two desires influence one behaviour. Such an approach clearly goes against the moral position that Kant advocated regarding beneficence: that an act cannot have any moral worth if there are motives other than reason at work, such as selfish ones and/or those based on desire. But to make the point again, motivational pluralism is a descriptive thesis – it does not suggest how we should act, but rather seeks to explain how we have evolved to act the way we do. The example they give is that it is more suitable to have altruistic beliefs about promoting one's children's welfare, as these tend to produce action and can be projected into the future, than hedonistic ones (such as a parent who feels bad about their children) since these may or may not produce the action required and are transient. With no beliefs attached to the feeling, each occasion has to generate a new response. The hedonist requires both a belief that their children require help and the belief that the action will promote pleasure and diminish pain. Sober and Wilson conclude that in this case, altruism is more reliable than hedonism in securing parental care for offspring. Likewise for the second type of pluralism. Here hedonism alone loses out, as having both altruistic (my children need help) and egoistic (helping my children serves my interests) motives available maximize the chances that the action will occur, thus most likely benefiting the children. The demands made on us by our human environments have resulted in us evolving to be motivational pluralists, argue Sober and Wilson. Their view does not quite bridge the gap between evolutionary, psychological and moral altruism, but it certainly narrows it. Moreover, their idea of motivational pluralism complements the complexities demanded by Boehm's insights, where social interactions make a range of demands on an agent.

In this chapter we have considered how altruism, as a behaviour, might have evolved and we have considered arguments in the philosophy of biology that both support and oppose the very possibility of altruism. We have seen how an evolutionary explanation of altruistic behaviour offers insights into our understanding of how we have come to act in the way that we do, but that the evolutionary account, though plausible, is not without its problems. Further, no descriptive account of the origins of our motivations, no matter how detailed, can instruct us on what we *ought* to do, and in particular on what kinds of altruists we should aspire to be. This is still the preserve of philosophy. We shall return to these questions in the final chapter. In the next chapter, however, we consider an alternative explanatory paradigm for human altruism: the social psychological one.

4

The altruistic personality

Explaining altruism psychologically

We saw in the last chapter, how evolutionary approaches to altruism explain it only by evacuating it of its most distinctive component: the motivation to assist another. Altruism thus understood can be seen as simply a strategic form of self-interest, much as one might tolerate an objectionable person only to put oneself in a position where one could later ask them a favour. Self-interest is the default position. We no more seek to explain it than we worry why it is that people generally walk forwards. While we did encounter some accounts of evolutionary altruism that acknowledge there is such a thing as genuine altruistic behaviour, they have trouble bridging the gap between the explanation of such behaviour and moral motivation. In this chapter we survey the contribution of social psychology to the study of altruism. Here we have a body of work that tries to apply scientific rigour to the question of why people (sometimes at least) put others first.

Free from the narrative of species survival that tempts sociobiologists to explain altruism through an appeal to promoting genetic self-interest, one might expect psychologists to take a more sympathetic view of its reality. Some of them have, as we shall see, but altruism has been a bit of a puzzle for psychologists, too, since the main theories of human behaviour they have to hand make similar assumptions about self-interest (Krebs 1970; Monroe 1994: 878–83). Indeed, the idea that it is *altruism* which requires an explanation makes sense only against a background where it is assumed that most human behaviour is egoistic. 'The territory that has been allotted to altruism is no more than a quaint province in an egoistic empire', according to Batson (1991: 62). On the other hand, the everyday help and assistance that makes social life possible and sometimes pleasant can hardly be denied. The question is how to interpret it. Faced with the reality of people's altruistic behaviour, psychologists have reached for theories of social learning, arousal reduction, empathic identification and moral development, among others. Yet, as so often in the social sciences, investigators have differed not only in their preferred explanations, but also in those explanations' objects. The debates between psychologists about how to explain altruism illustrate the irreducible theory-ladeness of altruism as a social phenomenon, as well as the imperialistic ambitions of competing explanatory paradigms. In exploring the psychological approach to altruism, we will need to pay particular attention to the identity of the concept and the more philosophical question of what counts as an explanation.

Impressed by the fact that, in different domains and varying circumstances, some people consistently behave more altruistically than others, the social learning perspective seeks to understand why this is so (Rushton 1980, 1982). Key to the approach is the idea that individuals learn to be altruistic, much as they might learn any kind of behaviour. Some learning is mimetic: children observe adults and tend to copy their behaviour. If they observe altruism, they will tend to become altruistic. Other learning is effected through structures of reward and reinforcement. If altruism is associated with pleasant feelings it will tend to be reproduced socially. People also learn things because they are told them by people in a position of authority (teachers, preachers or politicians) or because they imbibe the messages of the wider public political culture. The advantage of this theory – 'the most prevalent approach to altruistic personality' according to one of its critics (Krebs and van Hesteren 1992: 142) – is the clear and simple strategy it recommends to increase the amount of altruism in society: improve socialization and pump out messages that praise 'pro-social' behaviour.

But social learning theory is beset by some serious problems. The notion of reinforcement has difficulty in explaining why anyone would be altruistic in the first place; in this respect its overriding focus on children is telling: their altruistic exemplars are conveniently present on the scene (Losco 1986: 325–7; Krebs and van Hesteren 1992: 142–4). The social learning approach is linked to Herbert Spencer's Social Darwinism, which we encountered earlier, through the idea that moral development (altruism included) ought to be promoted if it leads to greater pleasure. In both cases, values are simply read off behaviour. Another problem is that, notwithstanding its apparent focus on personality, the social learning perspective tends to minimize differences in people's character, upbringing and moral outlook. Personality becomes not, as we ordinarily use the term, something with a rather particular referent, but the locus on which social influences push.

Above all, however, behaviouristic approaches, such as social learning, simply bypass the issue of motivation. As we have been arguing all along, however, the latter is central to altruism. When one person does another a favour it may be quite important to know whether they want to do good, relieve guilt, achieve compliance, conform to a norm, reciprocate a prior favour or, ingratiate themselves with someone in a position of power (Krebs 1982).

Altruism is not there every time one person adds to another's well-being. (Here, we see some psychologists' tendency to define what we want to explain in terms that depend on the explanation.) What we need to do is to try to recover people's intentions, and having recovered them to examine what made them the way they are. This is not easy, but it should not be dismissed on methodological grounds. The behaviourist school, of which the social learning perspective is exemplary, spurned intentions because they were not scientific and they concentrated instead on what was. Their question is, what can we know with some certainty? But while it is understandable not to journey down a road whose destination is unknown, it is more problematic to take another route and then announce that this is where the first road led all along. Sometimes we have to accept that we can't get there.

Social learning theory articulates altruistic behaviour through people's possession of more or less stable personality traits. We can argue about whether the theory provides a convincing explanation of why actors have or lack altruistic traits, but the basic assumption that altruism is a matter of personality is plausible enough. It needs to be contrasted, however, with 'state' perspectives on altruism which interpret the phenomenon situationally in terms of the immediate social environment within which altruistic acts occur (or fail to occur). Our interest now shifts from persons to circumstances. Much of the debate over the explanation of/for altruistic behaviour, concerns the relative weight to give 'trait' or 'state' factors, as we shall see.

Emergency situations and the bystander effect

Some of the most interesting and widely cited research in the altruism literature focuses on 'state' not 'trait'. This concerns people's behaviour in emergency situations, when they are called upon to offer immediate help to a person in grave danger. Much of the stimulus for this work stems from the much discussed tragedy in 1964 that befell Kitty Genovese, a 29-year-old office worker who lived in New York. In March of that year, when returning home at 3 a.m. to her apartment block in Queen's, Genovese was murdered by Winston Moseley, a man unknown to her. Thirty-eight people, residents of the block, heard her frantically scream for help for over half an hour. None of them intervened, called the police or took other measures to alleviate the anxieties, which another human being's desperate cries for help provoke. The case became something of a media sensation.

The Genovese case distresses us because we all think someone should have helped, but no one on the scene was moved to do so. The norm of helping strangers in distress was not operative, and in considering why this was so it makes sense to look at other features of the situation at hand. (A trait perspective by contrast would direct us to look at the personalities of the bystanders, but this seems unhelpful as there is no reason to think they were anything but a normal cross-section of New York's apartment dwellers.) In their study, inspired by the Genovese case, Latané and Darley are sceptical of whether norms, contradictory, vague and unclear, are actually invoked by people making speedy decisions in extreme circumstances (Latané and Darley 1970: 26–8).

Their theory hinges on the peculiar demands made on us when our behaviour is public. Rescue of a distressed person offers, of course, the possibility of reward and esteem, but rescuing can also go wrong or be inappropriate (perhaps the victim is not in distress after all), making the actor liable to embarrassment or being publicly labelled a fool, not to mention the physical danger that can accompany rescue endeavours. Faced with such costs that bear upon the belief that one morally ought to respond, an individual in public situations looks to others for guidance. What they see, of course, are others in the same dilemma also looking for social cues. The result is the 'bystander effect' where, para-doxically, the presence of numbers of people serves to inhibit action by any one of them. This is more subtle than the thought that each person hopes that another will go to help; the thesis is rather that each is looking to others to tell them whether helping is the thing to do. In a series of experiments, Latané and Darley (1970) found that the more witnesses there were to the incident, the less likely subjects were to help, whether this was reporting smoke billowing into a room, alerting others to a very visible theft of money from an envelope left in a waiting room or assisting a distressed woman, whose screams could be heard from behind a screen, after she had apparently injured herself. The fewer people who heard the woman's screams, for example, the faster she got help: one witness, and help would come quickest of all.

It's worth noting that the public bystander phenomenon that exercised Latané and Darley, seems not quite what occurred in the Genovese case, since there the residents of the various apartments had little means of assessing their neighbours' reactions. As they note, however, if other's *can't* be observed then each may assume someone else is taking action (Latané and Darley 1970: 90–1). And when no one does help, the moral responsibility for collec-tive inaction is diffused among the group – a kind of censure which is easier to bear.

In Latané and Darley's case studies bystanders, faced with the cognitive dissonance of knowing at some level that help is required but being unwilling to render it, had a strong incentive to reinterpret the situation so as to persuade themselves that the emergency did not really exist. They came to believe that the smoke must be harmless, that the theft under their noses had not really taken place, and they led themselves to think that it would be inappropriate to help the distressed woman. At the same time, they consistently denied the effects that other bystanders' behav-iour had upon them. Generalizing on the phenomenon that bystanders seemed to make a conscious decision to help or not, Piliavin and her collaborators constructed a cost-arousal model of response to emergencies that built on Latané and Darley's results (Piliavin *et al.* 1981). Emergency situations are distinguished by a shortage of time and extreme danger – not just for the victim but often for their rescuer too. They visit on their witnesses fear, sympathy, anger and other unwelcome emotions. The Piliavin team took it as an axiom that witnesses experienced a strong motivation to reduce their heightened arousal. Practically speaking, they faced a choice of helping, going to fetch help, leaving the scene (likely to provoke self-blame and maybe censure from others) or rejecting the victim as undeserving of help.

The cost-arousal model hypothesizes that a bystander will choose the response that will most efficiently reduce their arousal – and, in the process incur as few costs (in time, money, distress and so on) as possible. If a distressed child could be rescued swiftly and without too much risk, a witness will do it, for example, and appreciate the praise their action will attract. Conversely, a person enjoying a pleasant reverie is unlikely to insert themselves in a dangerous situation – though they will likely experience some self-censure at their inaction. If the costs of both helping and not helping are high – perhaps someone is the only witness to a physical assault – they will tend to redefine the situation in ways which reduce their liability. Here thoughts like 'they deserved what they got', 'someone else will help' and so on, will arrive conveniently on their mental horizon.

The bystander effect, catalogued by Latané and Darley, is on this model more explicitly theorized as a cost-reduction mechanism. Indeed, subjects' self-centred concern with their own arousal means that even if they resolve to assist another, they are not genuinely altruistic, but rather motivated by 'a selfish desire to rid [themselves] of an unpleasant emotional state' (Piliavin *et al.* 1969: 298). In contrast to Latané and Darley, Piliavin's team also discuss some 'trait' factors that influenced helping. Thus, they noted that helpers tended to be more other-oriented, more extrovert and more in need of social approval than passive bystanders. There is some evidence that people prefer helping those who are racially similar, dissimilarity being theorized as an extra cost that helpers must bear (a point to which we shall return). Women are more motivated to help when the recipient seems more dependent: men, when physical strength is required.

The trait input, however, can only be taken so far. Too mechanical a connection between character and the decision to help and the cost-arousal model would become redundant. In this, as in all versions of the rational choice calculus, subjects are perceived as decision-makers at heart. Features of persons and their character (such as whether a person is racially similar) enter the model as costs or benefits for actors. Thus a more extrovert person might regard it as less costly to get involved in public than a more introverted one (although they may simply be more aware of their surroundings). This emphasis on self-interested choice is part of Piliavin's team's denial that genuine altruism is involved in emergency intervention. This is a little dispiriting, however. For while Pilavian and her collaborators investigate only one form of 'pro-social' behaviour, one might think that if altruism isn't present when people go to help victims of theft, assault, epileptic seizures, drowning and the like, then it is very unlikely ever to surface.

Altruism as empathy

In hypothesizing that subjects are irredeemably self-centred in attending to their own emotional states, Piliavin's rescuer has some similarities with what Karylowski (1984) has called *endocentric* altruism. Here a person is largely concerned with their moral self-image. This is in contrast to *exocentric* altruism where subjects exhibit a genuine other-regarding concern for the needs of the other, unadulterated by self-centred considerations. Karylowski maintains that both the endocentric and exocentric variants are genuine altruism, arguing that for an exocentric altruist it needn't matter whether it is they or another who assists the person in need. His endocentric altruist is a more moral type than Piliavin's arousal-aversive character for they are motivated not so much by their desire to avoid a negative emotional experience than by their wish to live up to self-legislated moral standards. This seems a bit more altruistic, though as we shall see later, there is evidence that while some altruists experience an immediate connection with those they assist, others act principally from more abstract moral standards, evidence which supports Karylowski's distinction between exocentric and endocentric altruism.

The fact remains, however, that Piliavin's cost-averse folk, Latané and Darley's norm-free cue-takers and Karyloswki's moralistic endocentric altruist are all preoccupied with their own responses to those in need and are thus, arguably, not wholehearted, other-directed altruists. Against this view, Batson (1991), in a number of experiments, has sought empirical confirmation of genuine altruism. In his view, a person's experience of another's suffering will, if they are altruistic, evoke in them an empathetic desire to relieve it. Batson does not deny that empathic motives may be accompanied by cost-aversive and reward-seeking behaviour. But his 'empathy-altruism hypothesis' claims that the latter does not contaminate a germ of pure altruism evident in the immediate empathic connection a person experiences on perceiving another in need of help. As Batson is well aware, the hypothesis is difficult to prove, given the stubborn presence of less salubrious motives that often accompany altruistic activity. One way would be to ask people what their motives for helping were, but the appeal of testimonial accounts is mitigated by the tendency of respondents to report rather loftier, more idealistic goals than those which in reality moved them to act. We have instead to infer motives from behaviour. By systematically varying the availability and attractiveness of different kinds of behaviour, Batson sought to isolate and identify motivational empathy.

In his experiments Batson provided other means by which subjects could secure the rewards, avoid the punishment or stop the aversive arousal that their altruistic action would bring. Thus in one series of experiments the subjects, all college students, were given the opportunity to befriend a lonely student who seemed in need of help (Batson 1991: 129–34). This empathetic act might well bring other benefits in its wake, friendship for the befriender, for example, or even a sexual relationship. By manipulating the situation so that the latter were not available, Batson was able to conclude that the befrienders were motivated by genuine empathy, tantamount to altruism. In fact, as he has more recently argued, people sometimes go to some lengths to avoid the social contact which would provoke altruism-inducing empathy (Batson 2002). Thus nurses, for example, may avoid too much social contact with the terminal patients in their care. Conversely, however, increased empathic understanding has improved care for vulnerable groups, such as AIDS victims, the homeless and ethnic minorities.

There seems to be a difference, however, between empathy in the real world and the empathic motivations of Batson's college student subjects in controlled conditions, and it is not clear that his theory can bridge this gap. The social world has a reality to it never quite reproduced in the laboratory (for one thing, it doesn't

include just college students). Further, as Monroe (2002) has
pointed out, there seem to be some cases where empathic involvement does not issue in altruistic endeavour. A sadistic or cruel
person, as opposed to one who harms others in more straightforward ways, has a kind of empathic knowledge of the world from
their subject's perspective. Conversely, there is certainly much
non-empathic (albeit usually endocentric) altruism, as when I put
a few coins in the charity collection tin out of a sense of social
duty.

Finally, in assessing Batson's work we encounter the question
signalled earlier of what genuinely counts as a social explanation
as opposed to a redescription in an alternative vocabulary. Is it
any surprise that empathic people are altruistic? Surely not.
However, despite these difficulties, Batson does seem to have
shown the reality of altruism proper, rather than simulacra pow-
ered by more self-serving motives. This is no insignificant result,
given the assumptions of Piliavin, Latané and Darley. It makes
Karylowski's exocentric altruist empirically credible and not a
fictive idealization. But the degree to which Batson has explained
why altruism occurs is a different matter. We might wish to ask
what sort of personalities have empathic traits and which have
not, as well as to 'state' questions about which kinds of real world
situations trigger their empathy, whether these are subject to
deliberate social intervention, and so on.

Explaining altruism through cognitive frameworks

A more causal account of human altruism, one not based on
artificial laboratory experiments, but capable, nonetheless, of
generating testable propositions has been developed over a
number of years by Krebs and van Hesteren (1992, 1994). They
argue that altruism can be explained in term's of a person's moral
development, through infanthood, childhood and adolescence,
terminating in a mature, adult moral consciousness. Such development is not an idiosyncratic matter, but involves instead the
progressive acquisition of cognitive structures of ever-increasing
reach and sophistication. Cognitive structures define a person's
moral world view, and an individual is only capable of the degree
of altruism that the stage structure they have presently reached
will allow. In formulating their model, Krebs and van Hesteren
rely upon Kohlberg's (1981) much discussed work on moral

development. For Kohlberg, moral reasoning begins with an awareness of punishment, motivating behaviour which avoids it. Next comes exchange and reciprocity; then conscientious conformity with social norms; then the recognition that others have rights as independent agents. Kohlberg's claim is that people progress through these stages in a set order, even if some people do not make the later stages.[1] Kohlberg's theory resonates with Christopher Boehm's anthropological approach, we mentioned in Chapter 3. Boehm similarly believes that morality may have developed in a social context as a response to punishment and as a means of conflict resolution.

Krebs and van Hesteren adapt Kohlberg's moral stage sequence to produce a stage theoretic account of forms of altruism. Thus individuals will progress from egocentric accommodation, to instrumental co-operation, to mutual altruism (aimed at fulfilling shared role obligations), to conscientious altruism (marked by a greater sense of social responsibility), to autonomous altruism (based on universal dignity, equality and rights for all). The final stage, not attained in reality except by a few moral saints, is a universal self-sacrificial love which echoes Kohlberg's speculative utopian stage where people are so integrated that the line between 'me' and 'we' is hardly drawn.

Krebs and van Hesteren maintain that people's altruism should qualitatively improve depending on the stage structure they have reached. To a large degree, this should correlate with age. Thus there is evidence that whereas toddlers are relatively self-centred, 6- and 7-year-olds will engage in reciprocal agreements, while by the age of 9 or 10, children are willing to help needy friends without any expectation of immediate return. By the time of adolescence, children will provide deeper sorts of emotional support for their friends. There is some evidence that people in later life help families, friends and neighbours to a disproportionate degree, although other research has suggested that 'helping can be a form of coping', in this case with the vulnerability induced by loss of parental and work-related roles (Midlarsky 1992). As people develop, according to Krebs and van Hesteren, the forms of behaviour they consider altruistic themselves become increasingly altruistic (as judged by their cognitive structures). The degree of consistency between ideals and behaviour that people aspire to achieve also becomes more stringent, and therefore, more consistent with others' interests and more altruistic.

Krebs and van Hesteren do not ignore the external environment: 'altruism results from an interaction between the stage structures available to people and the demands of the social and cultural contexts to which they are exposed' (Krebs and van Hesteren 1992: 160). Cognitive structures are more broadly based and constitutive than a personality trait like empathy. Adults who lack altruism, in their view, are immature, though they may change in the future. In contrast to both situational approaches, and Batson's empathy–altruism hypothesis, the emphasis of their cognitive development model is on characteristics of persons – their traits – explained by a general trajectory of progress.

It is important for us as parents, educators and citizens, to note that children gain in moral maturity as they become progressively more able to take the perspective of the other. However, although they acknowledge the influence of environmental factors which enable or inhibit the acquisition of cognitive structures, Krebs and van Hesteren say little about how these interact with people's progress through moral stages. But without more knowledge their model would seem unable to account for the differences between male and female helping, people's preference for assisting those similar to themselves, aversive arousal and other phenomena of altruism. Monroe also points to extreme cases of seemingly selfish individuals who suddenly display a capacity for altruism, such as Oskar Schindler who used his business acumen to save Jews in Nazi Europe and, conversely, selfless types who under pressure fail to show the altruism expected of them, such as Pope Pius XII who tellingly failed to speak out against the Nazis (Monroe 2002: 111).

Cognitive structures are general categories, but people can perceive their circumstances and judge what to do in quite idiosyncratic ways. Thus cognitive structures may not be of that much utility in predicting whether a particular individual in a particular instance behaves altruistically. People act (or fail to act) for their own reasons, and we all like to think we are better than we are. Sometime we censure ourselves for not expressing the altruism we believe we ought to have done, a phenomenon that drives a wedge between a person's cognitive structure and the behaviour they manifest in particular circumstances. It is unclear, therefore, how much predictive power the cognitive structure model really has.

As we noted, Krebs and van Hesteren's altruistic stages are reworked versions of Kohlberg's moral stages. Much the same sorts of behaviour would therefore be manifested by persons who are on the corresponding moral and altruistic stages. At one level, this is hardly a surprise: we would expect more moral types to be more altruistic and vice versa. But, at another, it elides the distinction worth holding on to between fulfilling moral requirements and more creative altruistic behaviour. The latter involves the motivation to improve the welfare of another in need, with little regard for whether one's own well-being is diminished. Most moral action, by contrast, is not directed in the first instance at its object's welfare, but in meeting one's duties. The difference may be a matter of motivation. I might sweep away the autumn leaves that have fallen from my tree onto my neighbour's front garden because I know they are busy and I think it a neighbourly thing to do. Or I might do my elderly friend's shopping in order to give their home help some time off.

These are undoubtedly altruistic acts, but (depending on the precise circumstances), moral philosophers would tend to see them as supererogatory, beyond strict duty. They might also jeopardize the performance of our basic moral obligations (suppose a person spends so much time helping their neighbour that they neglect their own family). We may here be reminded by Kant's insistence that we have moral obligations to ourselves and we have no obligation to be altruistic to the point of abject self-sacrifice or the neglect of others. Altruistic activity, therefore, need not result in a net moral benefit. As we have seen earlier in this book, the relationship between altruism and morality is a complex one, and a distinction between the two concepts is not always easy to draw. But Krebs and van Hesteren's model does not acknowledge this distinction. For them, altruism at the higher stages involves universal dignity, equality and rights. Altruists are just moral agents in good standing. The existence of altruism as a concept *sui generis*, related to but not reducible to morality, would seem to call for a parallel stage structure, casting doubt on the efficacy of their model.

The connection between altruism and morality is also relevant because of a further issue, not much explored by psychological (or indeed other) research on altruism: the perspective of the *recipients* of altruistic acts. The discretion that altruism seems to involve means that altruists may not direct their helping efforts to where they are most needed, or even to where they are needed at all. Taking the recipient's perspective seriously forces us to confront issues of status, hierarchy and self-esteem. Despite its immediate benefits, altruism may confirm recipients in their powerlessness, and do nothing to challenge social hierarchies and people's beliefs about their own passivity.

One writer has argued that, regardless of altruists' motivations, altruistic activity always enhances the donor's power and reduces that of the recipient (Worchel 1984: 386). That may be too sweeping, but it remains true that being the beneficiary of an altruistic act may confirm a person's sense that, this time at least, they are incapable of helping themselves. Rosen has found that people at the bottom of a status hierarchy are more likely to acquiesce to offers of unwanted help than those further up (Rosen 1984: 364). Moreover, altruism has the potential to degrade, stigmatize and foster resentment even among those who are, on balance, grateful for the assistance they receive. Nadler and Fisher mention war veterans, the aged and welfare recipients in this context (Nadler and Fisher 1984: 398). The stigmatizing effect of selective welfare benefits is sometimes cited as an argument for their universalization, as in basic income schemes. Worschel, and Nadler and Fisher, hypothesize that recipients of altruism, who thereby lose power, will try to restore some equity by helping a third party themselves. If this claim were true, altruism would often set in motion a chain reaction. In any case, these issues of power and hierarchy show that altruism is not an unconditional good, even if it is a universal one.

Good Samaritanism, friends and strangers

An intriguing example of misplaced altruism comes from Darley and Batson's (1973) recreation of the parable of the good Samaritan with seminary students in 1970s America. Students were asked if they would give a talk to visitors on a career in the priesthood. On their way to do so, they encountered a man slumped on the ground, apparently in some distress. Forty per cent of students offered the man help, but when manipulated into believing they were late for their talk, only 10 per cent helped. When the topic of their talk was the good Samaritan parable instead, 53 per cent helped. A significant minority, therefore, literally stepped over a man in distress on their way to give a talk about the good Samaritan! Somewhat charitably, Darley and Batson interpret these volunteers as being in a state of conflict: they did notice the man but they had also made a commitment to someone else to be somewhere and give their talk. They found that the most doctrinally rigid believers were least likely to help. The most likely to help were students whose religious belief grew out of their personal search for meaning in the world. This result is consistent with Batson's later work which sees the source of altruism as being in empathy.

The original good Samaritan was particularly virtuous because he helped a *stranger* in need: most people like to help others like themselves. Our predilection for similarity seems to have a natural sociobiological basis. Helping fellow members helps guarantee the group's survival and augments group solidarity as a by-product. Mutual helping confirms groups in their groupness (Miller 2004). Small communities are, as one would expect, more altruistic – this may also be due to the greater ease with which altruistic activity can be communicated through the group. Milgram (1970) argued that the relative indifference city dwellers displayed towards one another could also be explained by their need to avoid the cognitive overload that living cheek by jowl with a multitude of others involved. Small communities are less tolerant of deviants, however; city dwellers show less variation between helping deviants and those who belong than do their small town cousins. Forty-four per cent of residents of Tulsa, Oklahoma, mailed a (deliberately) lost envelope to a neutral address, while 53 per cent of residents in a nearby town did the same. But when the envelope was addressed to the 'Friends of the Communist Party', 25 per cent of Tulsa residents still mailed it on, but only 3 per cent of townsfolk did (Hansson and Slade, 1977).

Other research has confirmed that people prefer helping those with whose opinions they agree (Staub 1978: 315–8). There is some evidence from America that blacks are more inclined to help others than whites, but the issue is a complex one and much depends on the perceived responsibility of a person for their distress, the level of involvement that helping will entail, as well as white people's desire not to be seen as racist (Staub 1978: 320–5). All research on similarity is hindered by the fact that (dis)similarity works on several dimensions. If a white male driver helps a white female driver whose car has broken down, it may be hard to know how far this is due to their racial similarity and how far to male motorists' preference for helping distressed females over another man. The latter, of course, is an exception to the similarity hypothesis and shows there are other norms at play. The interpretation of the similarity claim must also be treated with some care. What counts as a similar trait is not a natural fact, but socially constructed and maintained (Kohn 1990: 70–1). Individuals have multiple, competing and overlapping identities, and who is in and who is outside the group is not fixed absolutely, rather it is partly a function of contingent circumstances. The person in distress might be separated by nationality, but in other circumstances be a fellow European; the beggar you choose to give a few coins to in India might be of a similar age to your own children. Further, altruistic behaviour can solidify group boundaries, suggesting a more complex picture where felt similarity is in part caused by prior interaction and not just the other way around. This fact will have some significance when we come to consider, in the next two chapters, how altruistic norms may be strengthened and encouraged. In addition, the similarity claim is more salient when, as in most instances of altruism, the potential beneficiaries are not in acute need. The stranger you ignore has less of a complaint if their needs are moderate; perhaps in time their fellows may help them. In emergency situations, similarity loses significance, both morally speaking and in fact (Piliavin *et al.* 1981: 144–5). Emergency intervention is not immune to judgements of responsibility, but high need beneficiaries have a good chance of getting help even from someone the other side of the social spectrum.

Rescuers of Jews in Nazi Europe

One of the most discussed cases of altruistic activity is distinguished precisely by the lack of prior social connection between helpers and helped. These are the rescuers of Jews in Nazi Europe: researched by several scholars but none more comprehensively than by Samuel and Pearl Oliner whose work, *The Altruistic Personality* (1988), has become a reference point for subsequent explorations of altruistic behaviour. Approximately 200 million people lived under Nazi occupation and, besides being subject to tyrannicide themselves, witnessed the genocide of European Jews. Estimates of those who sought to help vary widely, from about 50,000 to at the very most 500,000 (or 0.5 per cent) of Europe's population. The actions of this tiny minority put themselves under extreme risk. Death for themselves, their families and, of course, the Jews they tried to save, was the punishment expected and, very often, administered. (As a result, many rescuers tried to keep their activities secret from their families.) Despite these exceptional conditions, rescuers helped Jews obtain the necessities of life as they were progressively segregated and isolated; they freed them, where possible, from imprisonment; they harboured them behind false walls and in deserted outbuildings, helped them to maintain an underground existence; and, in many cases, they smuggled them to safety.

In different occupied countries distinguished by different historical contexts, physical locations and political conditions, rescue was made more or less difficult and it assumed different forms. Eighty per cent of Danish Jews survived the war, smuggled out of the country on boats bound for neutral Sweden. A tradition of religious tolerance in the Netherlands and Belgium, and the reluctance of locals to turn on Jews living in their midst in Italy and Bulgaria meant, proportionately, fewer were murdered. German, French, Rumanian, Hungarian and, above all, Polish Jews were the least likely to survive. Situational factors, however, only begin to explain rescue efforts since in all countries under occupation only a small minority actively intervened – despite the near-universal hostility Nazi occupation invoked in local populations. The investigation the Oliners and their team undertook could hardly have been more thorough. Four hundred and six rescuers were interviewed, together with 150 survivors and 126 non-rescuers (a misleading term that refers, not to bystanders but, to those engaged in other sorts of resistance activity). Interviews were followed-up with detailed questionnaires to build up a picture of the altruistic personality.

The Oliners found that many factors which one might think relevant in explaining helping behaviour in extreme conditions turned out not to be so. Religion, for example, was only weakly correlated with rescue activity. Thus deeply religious Polish Catholics took considerable risks to smuggle essentials to the ghettos, despite the longstanding tradition of anti-semitism in Poland. Nearly 70 per cent of rescuers had lived among Jews, but so too had over 50 per cent of bystanders, hardly convincing proof of the thesis that prior interaction triggered empathic feelings. Most rescuers were relatively apolitical. More than half of them had no pre-war acquaintance with the Jews they helped. About two-thirds of rescuers helped once they were asked; one-third took the initiative. One might conclude from this that the majority of non-proactive rescuers were not quite as heroic: having been asked, they did not feel they could refuse. That may to some degree be true – rescuers were human beings after all and reported feelings of resentment alongside feelings of responsibility. The Oliners conjecture, however, if few bystanders were asked only to refuse, that is because they had indicated by their word, deed or attitude that they were unlikely to be receptive to such requests. (At a mundane level, a person might process similar sorts of signals in deliberating about which neighbour to ask a favour.) The fact that so many were in a position to help, but did not is what ultimately defeats explanations based on situation and circumstance. Every environmental factor that might seem to pick out rescuers alone could be applied equally to their more passive fellows. Exploring rescue, therefore, leads us away from the situation and towards rescuers' personalities and their deepest self-conceptions.

One thing which distinguished rescuers was a belief in their own agency. They had faith that they were able to make a difference. While bystanders were equally hostile to the Nazis, rescuers alone had the confidence to take matters into their own hands. 'Rescuers did not simply happen on opportunities for rescue; they actively created, sought, or recognised them where others did not' (Oliner and Oliner 1988: 142). While fear and despair turned bystanders in on themselves in a self-centred bid for survival, rescuers pushed hard on the levers of possibility that they could reach. What motivated them was a basic value orientation learned from their parents. Rescuers regarded themselves as part of humanity in a way non-rescuers did not. 'My father said the whole world is one big chain', reported Johan, a Dutch rescuer. 'One little part breaks and the chain is broken and it won't work anymore' (1988: 142).

Rescuers did not regard Jews as especially deserving. What mattered was that they were people in need. Bystanders were more subject to negative stereotyping of Jews, whereas rescuers typically reported that '[f]or us, people were just people' (1988: 150). Bystanders' parents taught them to get on in life. Decisions were taken, consequences borne. Practical competence was

placed in the service of economic success. The instrumental
virtues of thrift and self-reliance were instilled at the expense of
intangible objects, such as feelings, values and ideas. However,
the self-preoccupation which might be regarded as a functional
attitude for participants in a competitive economic system, left
bystanders without the means to reach outwards under extreme
conditions. Their upbringing was more conformist, stressing
obedience. As children, they were more likely to be chastized and
punished by their parents, including physically punished. Rescuers by contrast were raised in a more tolerant, less deferential
atmosphere. Sanctions visited by their parents were always
accompanied by explanation and love. Above all, rescuers were
taught to care, to look outwards, to think of themselves as
responsible for fellow members of the human family, links in
Johan's father's chain.

Rescuers, however, were not all of the same type. Some were
principally motivated by the close contact with Jews they had
enjoyed prior to the war. They helped their friends and neighbours. Others, 37 per cent in the Oliners' report, were empathic:
they felt a direct connection with people in need and were aroused
by compassion, sympathy and pity. Fifty-two per cent were
normocentric. For normocentric altruists, the felt experience of
others' suffering was not enough on its own. This suffering was
also a violation of the norms of a reference group with which they
identified. The persecution of the Jews offended the values of
their family, church or community, and it was this which moved
them to act.

This seems to have occured most often with collaborative
efforts at rescue. Danish rescuers who together put Jews on boats
bound for Sweden were able to tap into a long-standing resentment towards a southern neighbour who had always looked set to
invade their small, flat, homogenous country. Nevertheless, normocentric rescuers were less personally involved with their
charges than empathic ones. Less involved still were principled
rescuers, the Oliners' final category which comprised just 11 per
cent of rescuers. Their motives were abstract: rescuing reaffirmed
their moral principles. Suzanne helped several hundred people,
none of whom she knew, finding them jobs in agriculture and
domestic work where they were unlikely to be detected. She had
had little contact with Jews before and seems not have been

moved in the first instance by their suffering. 'All men are equal and all are born equal by right', was the only motive she reported (Oliner and Oliner 1988: 203).

Most rescuers did not regard themselves as having made a choice. They rarely deliberated before acting, and many reported that what they did was ordinary even though it patently was not. They were, in the psychological jargon, 'extensive personalities'. The closeness, care, reasonableness, lenient punishment and high moral standards that marked their upbringing, left them with values of personal responsibility, self-reliance, trust, openness to others and integrity. Bystanders experienced weak family attachments, strong discipline, and an atmosphere of insecurity, anxiety and suspicion. This left them 'constricted' personalities. Interestingly, in a piece of research conducted some time before the altruistic personality project, Rosenhan (1970) reached similar conclusions about US civil rights activists. White liberal activists committed to the black civil rights cause in 1963–5, when being so was likely to lead to stigma, were found to come from healthy, stable families based on mutual respect and an awareness of others' needs. The less than fully committed, perhaps equivalent to the Oliners' non-rescuers, described their parents in negative or ambivalent terms.

What comes across powerfully, reading the Oliners' testimony, is that rescuers 'were and are "ordinary" people'.

> They were farmers and teachers, entrepreneurs and factory workers, rich and poor, parents and single people, Protestants and Catholics. Most had done nothing extraordinary before the war, nor have they done much that is extraordinary since. Most were marked neither by exceptional leadership qualities nor by unconventional behaviour. They were not heroes cast in larger than life molds. What distinguished them were their connections with others in relationships of commitment and care ... Their involvement with Jews grew out of the ways in which they ordinarily related to other people.
>
> (Oliner and Oliner 1988: 259–60)

The scale and ambition of the Oliners' work has meant it has attracted much comment. Kohn believes the Oliners missed an opportunity to reflect on whether men (with arguably greater self-esteem and assertiveness) or women (with perhaps more empathy and guilt) helped more (Kohn 1990: 81–2). Krebs and van Hesteren express some scepticism whether testimony, 40 years after the event, accurately reflects the motives that rescuers had at the time (Krebs and van Hesteren 1992). Similarly, Batson doubts that testimony, even if accurate, really reported altruistic motives. A rescuer who said, for example, that 'I didn't think I could live with that knowing that I could have done something' seems, on Batson's schema be motivated by a desire to avoid shame and guilt; neither, according to him, truly altruistic motives (Batson 1991: 182). Similarly a person who reported that they could not bear what the Nazis had done to the Jews could well be interpreted as acting on aversive arousal. This seems a little churlish, however, and arguably reveals more about the limits of Batson's model than it does the Oliners' conclusions.

A more apposite critique questions whether all the rescuers were genuinely moved by altruism. They were of course altruistic in their deeds, they rescued others' lives taking great risks in the process and on one definition that is enough. It does not suffice, however, if motivation is the distinctive feature of altruism because both the evidence presented and theoretical reflection may cause us to doubt whether every rescuer was an altruist. We have already encountered Suzanne, who kept her distance from those she assisted, and reported that what caused her to act was the denial of rights that the Nazi persecution of the Jews involved. However, it is not clear that the majority (52 per cent) of normocentric rescuers had altruistic intentions either. Like the principled rescuers, they had no direct connection with their victim and were moved by a sense of obligation to their reference group. What of the 37 per cent of empathic rescuers? Only they, we might say with Batson, were moved by the direct empathic connection they felt for another human being. Moreover, as other commentators have pointed out, all three types of rescuers, simply by their actions asserted moral values distinct from altruism.

Blum mentions resistance to evil, anti-racism, and affirmation of the distinctive worth of the Jewish culture (Blum 1992: 36–42). Konarzewski (1992), citing evidence that 17 per cent of rescuers declared their hatred of the Nazis as a reason for acting, points to political protest as a motive not only distinct from empathic identification, but in some tension with it. But, again, we might say if rescuing Jews was not altruistic then nothing is, and any argument which doubts their altruism might seem on that account defective. People like Suzanne who acted purely from moral principle were surely a small minority. As their testimony shows, the great majority of rescuers did act out of a sense of compassion and empathy, whatever other more disinterested moral motives they might also have had. The plight of the Jews provided them with an opportunity to put latent moral and group-based norms into action. It may seem over-simple to divide up the wartime population of Europe into a majority of 'constrictive' and a small minority of 'extensive' personalities, but the latter may be distinguished not by the moral beliefs they held but by their willingness to affirm them in extreme circumstances (Churchill and Street 2004). Only a minority of people were brought up to have such faith in their own beliefs. Altruists are people who actually do good in the world and do not just think it or hope it happens.

'A common humanity'

Monroe's (Monroe *et al.* 1990; Monroe 1996) work on rescue behaviour reveals findings somewhat similar to the Oliners', but also divergent in some significant respects. Like the Oliners, she found that rescue behaviour could not be explained by the psychic well-being it occasioned or by a need to atone for past wrongs or by any cost-benefit calculation (Monroe *et al.* 1990: 110–5). Nor could the decision to rescue be explained by religious affiliation, birth order and – here she departs from their conclusions – there was no consistent connection in relations with parents or other role models (Monroe 1996: 130–5). Like them, she believes rescuers and bystanders had sharply contrasting personalities and it is these personality differences that she believes are the key to an explanation. Non-rescuers had less faith in their own agency, they were less resourceful, and saw themselves as helpless, isolated individuals who could do little to combat Nazi power. Monroe's rescuers, like the Oliners', came from all walks of life. On the surface, they exhibited a wide variety of personality types. They all felt a greater connectedness with humanity, however, and some, though by no means all of them, felt that their altruism had been inculcated through their upbringing. Time and again, Monroe's interviewees downplayed their rescue activity. None of them believed their behaviour was out of the ordinary, despite the mountain of evidence to the contrary, and all of them believed they only did what anyone else would have done.

These beliefs are key to Monroe's construction of an alternative explanation of the rescue of Jews based on a distinct perceptual framework possessed by only the small minority of rescuers (and other altruistic individuals who similarly risked their lives to save others). In contrast to the Oliners, Monroe sees rescuers distinguished, not so much by group ties, norms or the possession of a particular set of moral beliefs – indeed she stresses how altruists did not necessarily have a better moral character than non-altruists (Monroe 1996: 184–5, 197–9) – but, by their perception of a shared humanity, the overriding belief that at base individuals are all fellow members of the family of human beings. When faced with a person in dire need, rescuers did not see a stranger, a Jew, or, for that matter, a neighbour, but simply a fellow member of humanity. 'You help people because you are human,' reported Bert, a Dutch rescuer (Monroe 1996: 197).

Indeed rescuers regarded themselves as having no choice but to harbour Jews and assist them in a myriad of other ways. Rescue was a pre-reflective action, a reflex on perceiving that a fellow human being was in need. The powerful feelings which moved them to act together with a cognitive framework that explained the meaning of the wrong committed combined or, perhaps better, transcended the traditional division between reason and passion in human nature (Monroe 1996: 213–4, 234). (This seems not so dissimilar to the motivational pluralism of Sober and Wilson, we encountered in Chapter 3.) Be that as it may, rescuers did not have a loftier or more optimistic view of human nature than bystanders, and they were not judgemental. Though they did express hostility to the Nazis, they did not see the Jews as especially worthy and, in their daily conduct, they did not divide people into good or bad. For the rescuers, people were people, with common needs and vulnerabilities.

This contrasted with another group that interested Monroe: entrepreneurs. While the entrepreneurs she interviewed donated significant sums to charity, and thus were arguably altruistic to some degree, they tended to give to causes with which they were personally associated. Thus, entrepreneurs had a strong sense of group loyalty, by contrast with rescuers who regarded other people, neighbours, strangers, Jews, and even Nazis simply as human beings. The rescuers' world view contrasts sharply with the rhetoric of dehumanization used by perpetrators of genocide worldwide. The ties that bind together human beings were, for rescuers, a basic ontological fact about our existence on earth, more permanent than the result of any human endeavour. Like John Donne, they believed that '[a]ny man's death diminishes me because I am involved in mankind' (cited in Monroe 1996: 204).

In sharp contrast to the calculating individualist of rational choice theory (a character whom we shall encounter in the next chapter), rescuers of Jews deliberated little, set aside their own well-being and saw themselves as inextricably tied to a larger collective. Indeed, their affinity with others provides an interesting parallel with Emile Durkheim's investigation of altruistic suicide, in his famous nineteenth-century treatise (Durkheim [1897] 1970: 217–40). Subjecting the available data on suicide in the late nineteenth century to close scrutiny, Durkheim maintained that it could be categorized into one of three classes. While egoistic and anomic suicides arose from too little social integration, altruistic suicides were the pathological result of too much. Durkheim catalogued the many ancient and medieval societies which positively demanded the suicide of their members in certain social circumstances, such as the death of one's chief (among certain Gallic tribes) or a woman's husband in India (the practice of *sati*). Sometimes suicide was not strictly required but was a good way of acquiring social prestige. It was popular among Hindu Brahmin, for example. A Brahmin of a certain age who had left at least one son could confirm his high status by taking his own life.

Of particular interest for Durkheim were suicides in armies. Statistics for every European country in the mid- to late-nineteenth century showed suicide rates among serving soldiers to be far higher than among the civilian population. Durkheim explained this by likening armies to ancient tribes. A soldier in nineteenth-century France had to accept their superiors' impositions, renounce their own interests and set little store on their own life, much as did the Gallic warrior who was their forebear. Only the affinity between armies and 'primitive' peoples could explain why soldiers took their lives for the most trivial of reasons, such as being refused leave or promotion. While egoistic suicide was accompanied by depression and melancholy, altruistic suicide required a burst of faith, an energetic enthusiasm for one's social group.

Durkheim's suicides have, in common with Monroe's, altruists a tendency to ignore the division between self and others. Both of them set aside self-centredness to serve the interests of a larger group. It is true that altruistic suicide may not seem that altruistic (or indeed that moral), although perhaps the immediate family of a tribe member who took their own life might gain some vicarious prestige. It is also true that the boundaries of one's group are smaller than that of humanity at large; what is so praiseworthy about many rescuers of Jews is that religious difference meant nothing to them. But, divided by a century, what both Durkheim and Monroe catalogue is the sense of connection one consciousness has with others and the subordination of individual interests.

Notwithstanding this, there does seem to be a large discrepancy between Monroe's champions of a common humanity and more everyday altruism (such as that of her entrepreneurs) where group ties are important. As we have seen, more mundane altruists are motivated to a degree by their felt similarity with the person in need. People reciprocally like to help those who have something in common with them, such as their race or religion, for example. How do we square this well established result with rescuers of Jews, many of whom were strangers to them? The Oliners get round this problem simply by defining altruism as helping behaviour that is inclusive and that disregards traits, such as race, gender or religion (Oliner and Oliner 1988: 6–7). But while helping strangers may be a more admirable form of altruism there seems no reason to classify 'in-group' altruistic behaviour as, by that token, non-altruistic.

One possible explanation for the discrepancy between people's preference for helping similar others and gentile rescuers of Jews comes from evolutionary biology. If groups with shared traits *reciprocally* assist each other then we might explain this in evolutionary terms as a means to group survival. But not all altruistic assistance is reciprocal and not all traits are genetic in origin (religion, for example) – besides which, the explanation is weakened by the problems associated with the whole genetic approach as discussed in the last chapter. The better solution is the more straightforward one. The rescue of Jews and the more everyday altruistic endeavour (donating money, volunteering time, offering skills, helping injured strangers and so on) are simply two different types of activity. In the second, more common cases, people are more strongly motivated to help those they feel some connection with, though they are prepared to help strangers too. This explanation fits our intuition that rescuers were exceptional and the fact that they were a small minority. Not everyone has faith in a common humanity, and, if the Oliners are correct, only a minority of people were fortunate enough to have the kind of upbringing which led them to see the world that way. It captures our sense that while most of us are prepared to offer time and resources to others up to a point, we have our limits, and, if we are honest, few of us would have taken the risks that these rescuers did. It also illustrates a point that Monroe stresses: altruistic behaviour exists on a continuum from greater to lesser, and not all behaviour belongs to either the altruism category or the self-interested (Monroe 1996: 16–8).

At the same time, however, the claim that rescue behaviour is just a more (perhaps the most?) extreme form of altruism seems unsatisfactory, for the *continuum* between more and less altruistic behaviour sits oddly with the *division* between group-based motivation and the belief in humanity at large. Groups have boundaries which stop short of a common humanity and part of what membership of a group involves is an awareness of the contrast between members and non-members. These contrast effects are an important part of solidarity in all groups, though also a source of intergroup enmity: a person is a Protestant and not a Catholic, a Hutu and not a Tutsi. But with the idea of a common humanity these contrast effects do not exist. What is important is not the division between one's group and another but simply our common membership of the human family. The point is that one cannot get from group membership to membership of a common humanity just by progressively expanding the size of one's group. For if groups rely on contrast effects then there will always be an 'out-group' that contrasts with one's 'in-group'. To believe in the family of human beings, as opposed to one's religious or ethnic 'family', requires a kind of gestalt shift, a fundamental change in one's perceptions. And that basic difference is inconsistent with the perception of rescue activity as simply a more extreme form of the same kind of helping behaviour we can observe around us in our everyday lives. Based on this argument, Monroe's position could only be saved by recategorizing rescue as something fundamentally different from normal helping, a form of altruism that transcends what we normally regard as altruistic activity. If that were the case, then the common humanity explanation would simply not apply to many cases of altruism.

There is a further issue. Whatever the merits of the common humanity explanation for altruism, it raises the question of what explains the fact that it is a world view shared by only some. What explains its less than frequent occurrence? Earlier we criticized Batson's empathy-altruism hypothesis for being an incomplete explanation for altruism. To say that altruistically motivated people experience empathy is not insignificant, but it seems also a redescription of what altruism involves – at least if all genuine altruists are empathic. A similar criticism might be levelled at Monroe. Belief in a common humanity might be the ground of altruism, but we want to know what grounds the ground, or more accurately what causes it. Here she offers only a brief speculation. '[T]he particular perspective that constitutes the heart of altruism might easily be activated by many different factors, from genetic coding and religious teachings to group or kinship ties and psychic utility' (Monroe 1996: 214). Different altruists will ultimately be motivated by different sorts of reasons. This is a little unsatisfactory, however. Neither Monroe nor the Oliners found evidence that rescuers had stronger group ties than bystanders (though admittedly on the Oliners' hypothesis the rescuers might have had stronger relationships with their more liberal parents); while psychic utility seems to construe a common humanity merely as an idea in which it is rewarding to believe. This leaves the not infeasible but hard to establish genetic coding explanation. Could the most altruistic of altruists have their brains hard-wired in a different way from the rest of us? It is not likely we will ever know.

Despite all this, there remains something tremendously attractive about the idea of a common humanity as the ground for altruism. It is not just the basic moral appeal of such a cosmopolitan idea. It is also the intuitive fit between behaviour that aids another and a world view that sees people as essentially connected. Moreover, if the common humanity explanation does not help that much in explaining why people like to help their own, perhaps it is still useful in accounting for the large quantity of altruistic endeavour that is not heroic and not directed at members of one's group. We pick up old people who have fallen down, return lost children to their parents, mail post that has been misdirected to us, donate blood without knowing the recipient, give directions to those who look lost, and so on. This small-scale real life altruism, helps maintain our faith in our fellow humans, and may do a little to foster trust between citizens.

However, there is no doubt that some are more willing to help than others, and it is not implausible to think that the more active helpers are animated by some belief in a common humanity that those less willing to help were not. At least, this claim has credibility when considered the other way around. It is plausible to think that the less altruistic of our fellow citizens have stronger beliefs about personal responsibility and self-sufficiency. In contrast to their more altruistic neighbours who see human beings as essentially connected, their basic ontology may be one where each of us is an isolated monad. Whether these sorts of values and beliefs are malleable and open to reform is an interesting question. In Chapter 6, we shall discuss the possibility of a political project aimed at improving people's motivationally relevant beliefs.

Rescuers of Jews in Nazi Germany, are probably the most studied group of altruists there are. Their courage and compassion continue to serve as a beacon of what humans beings can do at their best, a counterpoint to the horrors of the Nazis, and indeed to tyrants everywhere. Most of us would not have been so courageous. But today's societies offer many avenues for altruistic endeavour; there is never a shortage of needy strangers and grateful beneficiaries. Even if (as we shall explore in the next chapter) much need-fulfilment is institutionalized, there is always much good to be done and help to be given. In doing that good, and in the process cultivating in ourselves the altruistic virtues of care, compassion and empathy, we can do no better than be guided, as the rescuers were, by a belief in a common humanity. More than a slogan, it points towards an ethic of inclusion, equality and a refusal to condemn. Above all, it illuminates a vision of human beings bound together in their fates and their fortunes. As Tony, a Dutch rescuer from a wealthy family, puts it 'you should always be aware that every other person is basically you' (Monroe 1996: 205).

Notes

1　One reason Kohlberg's work is controversial is because he found that girls progress
　　higher up the stage sequence than boys. His former research student Carol Gilligan
　　argued that this is because females reason morally in a different (neither superior or
　　inferior) way than males. See Gilligan (1982).

5

Altruism, giving and welfare

We explored in the last chapter what sorts of people are altruists, their background and attributes, and whether anything can reliably be found that distinguishes their personalities from their more selfish fellows. The assumption behind all this was that altruism was a virtue: a good thing to be (sometimes the best). But notwithstanding the goodness they bring into the world, the focus all along was on the altruist and what sorts of dispositions they have as a person. Many times, however, the moral urgency of vulnerable people's needs (the old, the sick, the poor, the infirm, and so on) is great enough that we need to shift focus from agents to recipients; what's most important is making sure their needs are met. In contemporary liberal democracies the welfare state bridges the gap between needy individuals and the limits of their fellow citizens' readiness to give. Here, however, an important question arises. Once altruistic endeavours are codified, regularized and enforced through legal channels, is there still a space for genuine altruism?

We examined in Chapter 2 the conflict between individual discretion and an impartial concern for each person's interests at a fairly high level of abstraction. In this chapter we take up the same issue more concretely by exploring the roles of charity, justice, and welfare in today's market societies. Is the welfare state, we ask, an avenue for altruism or does it crowd out people's other-regarding motivations? After surveying the dominant paradigm of self-interest in economic thought – the backcloth to the societies in which almost all of us live – we look at the nature of people's philanthropic giving. We broach the issue of welfare by considering in some detail Richard Titmuss's ([1970] 1997) seminal, *The Gift Relationship*. Titmuss famously argued that a system of voluntary blood donation is an avenue for altruism, and that altruistic motivation, directed at fellow citizens who are nonetheless strangers, is the foundation of the welfare state. Others argue to the contrary that welfarism crowds out altruistic motivation. We side with Titmuss that blood and other non-marketable goods are an important expression of citizens' fellow-feeling in contemporary individualistic societies. It is too optimistic, however, for the welfare edifice to be built exclusively on foundations of altruistic fellow-feeling. There are also important duties of social justice that citizens ought to meet, whether they are motivated to do so or not.

Altruism and the economists

Contrary to what one might expect, many of the great economists, Smith, Pareto Edgeworth and Walras, for example, did discuss altruistic motivation. In Smith's case, at least, this was largely to dismiss it. 'It is not from the benevolence of the butcher, the brewer or the baker that we expect our dinner', he famously wrote in *The Wealth of Nations*, 'but from their regard to their own interest' (Smith [1776] 1976: 26–7). How can the Smith of *The Wealth of Nations* be squared with the same person who 17 years earlier argued in *The Theory of Moral Sentiments* for an expansion of our empathetic sentiments towards others? This question has been labelled by his interpreters, 'the Adam Smith problem' (Kolm 2000a: 16). In the case of contemporary economists there has, again perhaps surprisingly, been some interest in altruism. One writer even claims that 'thinking about the economics of altruism has contributed to the rethinking of economics' (Phelps 1975: 3) though another, more sympathetic to altruism, maintains that altruistic behaviour is a 'painful nuisance' for economists (Lunati 1997: 50). The latter view may be the more accurate one since the way economists have accounted for altruism has arguably said more about economic methodology than it has about altruism.

The orthodox view of the rational, economic agent regards them as a self-interested maximizer of their own utility. They choose that bundle of goods that will most increase their well-being, however they choose to define that. They are self-interested, but not necessarily selfish. The rational, economic agent may take as their well-being the well-being of others, but they are not interested in others' well-being for the sake of those others. At the most, others are sources of their own utility. What we have then is an individualistic picture of the universe where individuals co-operate if by doing so (for example, in a firm) they can mutually serve their individual utility functions; they cease to co-operate once they do not. It is also a universe empty of normative significance.

Rational, economic agents may sometimes act on the basis of what they think is best or right, but only insofar as moral norms enter their utility functions. There are no basic moral principles to structure their actions, as supplied by God, for example, or natural law, or Kant's categorical imperative. They are rational in the purely instrumental sense that they choose the best course of action for themselves, not in the substantive sense of meeting external moral requirements or even of being reasonable. It is interesting to compare this picture with Monroe's finding, discussed in Chapter 4, that altruists are moved by their sense of connection to a common humanity. There can be no substance to the idea of a common humanity in the universe of the rational, economic agent.

This picture, economists contend, is more realistic than the altruistic alternative when we look at how actual people actually behave. In fact, as has often been pointed out, a world of perfect altruists would be incoherent and self-defeating. Each would be exclusively concerned with others' interests, leaving individuals without any interests of their own. (Two altruists arguing over who should have the last seat on a bus: 'After you,' 'No, after you!') The rational, economic agent is also easier to use in formal mathematical modelling than a more complex picture of human beings which sees us as committed to others, as frequently irrational and led by our emotions, and at least sometimes as moral. This, however, has led to some curious results as economists have attempted to explain the more altruistic aspects of social life using the sparse methodological tools at their command (Monroe 1994: 864–70). The American economist, Gary Becker's *A Treatise on the Family* (1981), is exemplary in this regard. Altruism is more common in families than it is the economic market because altruistic behaviour is more efficient in the former than the latter, he maintains (Becker 1981: 299). Families tend to be smaller than economic enterprises and they contain a denser network of interactions between the different

members, both of these making other-regarding behaviour easier
to engage in. Moreover, marriage 'markets' tend to match altruistic folk with self-interested spouses who prefer to benefit from
their partner's altruism, creating a stable arrangement where both
gain in different ways. (Two altruists married to each other would
suffer from the 'after you' problem, and two people eager to
benefit from others' altruism would enjoy less utility than if they
married altruists.) Becker's spouses behave just like the theoretic
game agents we encountered in Chapter 3; indeed the theoretical
game and rational choice approaches to human behaviour are
essentially the same. There is no thought here that the prevalence
of altruism within the family could be explained by the moral
quality of the relationships which it contains.

At other times, however, economics has provided insights into
altruism not immediately obvious to other branches of social
science, especially when supported by a rigorous empirical analysis. Thus one writer conceives of families' willingness to marry
out their daughters to wealthy families as a way of buying
insurance for themselves in their old age (Stark 1995: 8, 13). Or
again, while on the face of it it is more rational for families in
developing countries to send sons rather than daughters abroad to
lucrative jobs since sons tend to earn more and, hence, have more
income to send, many families prefer to send daughters because
girls tend to remit a higher proportion of their income and thus in
many cases will secure a greater income stream for their parents
and siblings back home (Stark 1995: 74–7). The family is the
main area where economists interested in more pro-social motivations have been able to apply their theories.

A son's monthly remittance to his family back home, or a
wealthy family supporting their poorer in-laws, may seem like the
kind of behaviour that violates the self-interestedness axiom of
rational, economic man. But, in fact, it is not because the beauty
of this model is that any good or activity may in principle
contribute to a person's utility function. My winning the lottery
augments my utility, but so too does my donating my winnings to
a children's home; such is the parsimony of utility. Here then, is
one way that economists are able to account for more altruistic
behaviour. Its drawback is that it accounts for altruism only by
evacuating it of its distinctive content: a person's desire to assist
another for their own sake. We are all familiar with the well-worn
debate about whether, if I give money to a beggar, I am really

motivated by their interests or my own desire to feel better about myself. If we take the latter course, we lose the ability to see altruism as a distinctive phenomenon: we are no longer able to regard some acts as more self-interested and others as more altruistic, with a continuum between the two. But there is surely an important difference (not least to the beggar) between my donating money to the beggar and deciding to keep it. Economists have tried to account for this difference by exploring the different kinds of utility that may lie behind apparently altruistic acts. For example, some altruistic acts may be motivated by a desire for reputation or for others' social approval: one might want to be seen as philanthropic. Others tend to reinforce a certain status hierarchy, such as parents helping their children. Still others, may be motivated by fear: Collard gives the example of employees accepting 'voluntary' wage restraint when there is the unspoken understanding that redundancy threatens if they do not (Collard 1978: 4–5). What reputation, status and fear have in common is that they see that agent taking a more enlightened, long-term or strategic view of their own self-interest than whatever immediate gains may lie within their reach.

Are economists right to assume that individual self-interest is the prevailing motive in social life? The problem, as we have seen, is that given a sufficiently capacious view of self-interest, virtually any kind of behaviour can be defined in terms of it. In a well-known article, the economist Amartya Sen labels this assumption 'definitional egoism' and argues that it conflates a person's choices with their welfare through the stipulation that no rational person would ever choose a course of action that lowers welfare over one that promises higher welfare (Sen 1977). Sen uses the term 'commitment' to describe the deliberate choice of a lower welfare stream. Commitment is involved in a person's decision to work hard at their job when their doing so cannot be wholly explained by incentives, such as pay or even intrinsic rewards, such as job satisfaction: a person may simply be committed to their work. (Perhaps this explains the position of aid workers in developing countries.) Another example is voting, something which those who subscribe to the rational, economic view have long found hard to explain. Why should a person take the trouble to vote when the chances of their being the decisive individual whose vote makes the difference are practically nil? Again, a person may be committed to a political party or even to their role as a citizen in the democratic system itself. Sen argues that to explain social phenomena involving commitment we have to move to a two-level view of agents where they choose not simply different sorts of preferences, but also consider the relative merits of alternate preference rankings. At the more evaluative meta-level, a person might deliberate over whether they prefer careers which promise a high income to those which serve causes dear to their heart, or whether to focus on meeting their duties as a parent or as an employee. The meta-level of preference formation drives a wedge between preferences and behaviour by explaining how individuals reflect on their behaviour, and it opens a space for genuinely non-self-interested altruism where a person resolves to commit themselves to a cause that may hardly benefit them personally at all. It also points towards a more complex picture of human beings in contrast with 'purely economic man' who is 'close to being a social moron' (Sen 1977: 37).

Reciprocity, exchange, and *The Gift*

In one area of social life, however, the rational, economic agent seems not to be moronic: they are able to engage in *reciprocal* relationships. As we saw in Chapter 2, reciprocity is a subtle phenomenon because it seems to be a sort of hybrid, somewhere between pure altruism and pure self-interest. Perhaps because of this, it is ubiquitous in social life. One can give a fairly self-interested explanation for reciprocity: if I can supply you a good beyond your reach at fairly low cost to myself, and you can do the same, there are good reasons for us both to enter a reciprocal trading relationship. On the other hand, a self-interested agent might not believe another's assurance that they will reciprocate, and if both think that way, a stalemate will ensue where neither party is prepared to initiate the trade. Some economists have sought to get round this problem by defining altruism as trust that the other party will, in fact, reciprocate (Kolm 2000b). Altruism, in this view, is the willingness to make a sacrifice when one cannot be sure that one's partner, in interaction, will do so too. (An example here might be the first trade union in a round of pay negotiations which accepts the government's urging to freeze wages in order to reduce inflation.) Moreover, for economists, the appeal to trust has some significance because it is arguably a necessary foundation for effective market functioning. Reciprocity need not involve market relations, however, the regularity of exchange it involves can often cement deeper social relationships particularly if an element of ritual is involved. This latter insight was brilliantly explored in Marcel Mauss's classic of anthropology, *The Gift* (Mauss [1950] 2002). Mauss surveyed practices of gift-giving from ancient times to the present, and in many different societies. He is remembered particularly for his description of the social ceremonies of the *potlach* among native North American tribes, and the rather similar *kula* practised by Melanesian peoples. Both these ceremonies, involving banquets, dancing, speeches and festivals, had at their core the ritualized giving and return giving of gifts. If one chieftain gave another a mask or a belt on behalf of his tribe the latter had to reciprocate; in fact they had to offer in return a gift of greater value. Mauss's insight was to use these examples to show that, contrary to what anthropologists had believed, there were, throughout human history, no unreciprocated gifts; giving *always* establishes an expectation of return. In his *Argonauts of the Western Pacific* (1932), Bronislaw Malinowski, classifying all the exchange relationships between the Melanesian Trobrian islanders, classed the regular presents a husband would give his wife as 'pure gifts'. But contrary to Malinoswki's view, Mauss argued that these were rather a payment for the sexual services she rendered him (Mauss [1950] 2002: 93). There are many other examples: what would you feel on your friend's birthday if they had unexpectedly given you a birthday present a few months before? '[W]hat creates the obligation to give is that giving creates obligation,' as one of Mauss's commentators has put it (Godelier 1999: 11).[1]

Mauss's work on the gift has a number of important implications. First, it blurs the distinction between social giving and economic selling and it thus enables us to see the economy – conceived of as established practices of exchange embedded in social life – as endemic throughout human history, and not a modern European invention. The chief difference between the gift economy and the market economy is that by:

> being more directly cued to public esteem ... the gift economy is more visible than the market [and] by being visible, the resultant distribution of goods and services is

more readily subject to public scrutiny and judgments of fairness than are the results of market exchange.

(Douglas 2002: xviii)

Second and relatedly, Mauss shows how reciprocal gift giving helps strengthen social bonds and promotes social integration. *Potlach* and *kula* ceremonies were rich with meaning and symbolism and involved the 'total social personality of the exchangers' (Davis 1992: 7, 78–9). Hobbes's vision of society as a war of every individual against every other, is domesticated by Mauss who for war substitutes the exchange of everything between everybody, as the anthropologist Marshall Sahlines argues (Sahlins [1972] 2004: 171–83). While this is a friendlier, more communitarian picture of social life than Hobbes's and the economists', Mauss also showed that social integration was quite compatible with hierarchies of status and prestige. As we noted, recipients were obliged to offer return gifts of greater value than those they had received (a further difference between the gift economy and the market economy). If a chief could not do so they lost face and were in the giver's debt. Thus although serving to integrate tribes who met at them, the *potlach* and *kula* also represented a perpetual struggle for social superiority – something, ironically enough, portended by Hobbes when he identified the quest for reputation as a cause of conflict (Hobbes [1651] 1996: 88). However, as a moment's reflection on the market economy will testify, there is nothing intrinsic to gift exchange that makes it rivalrous and antagonistic. In certain circumstances, counter-gifts have a similar value to original gifts, and where this occurs the participants in the exchange may be bound together in a mutually beneficial way. Thus when two men become double brothers in-law by each marrying a sister of the other's wife, they bind themselves together in a strong pact of mutual assistance which involves sharing goods between them, standing by the other in battle, and so on (Godelier 1999: 41). Thus, while gift exchange could be consistent with hierarchy and inequality, Mauss believed that mutually beneficial exchanges were more stable and morally preferable.

Charity, giving and justice

One problem with Mauss's work is that it seems in danger of obliterating altruism from social life. The more that recipients of gifts feel obliged to offer return gifts to their beneficiaries, the less we can see those beneficiaries as having genuinely altruistic motivations. It is hardly altruistic to be on the look out for a return gift. Moreover, the more that giving is ritualized, the less it is chosen, and hence the less it is an instance of creative altruism. As we saw in the last chapter, altruists regard themselves as connected to a common humanity and have strong feelings of empathy, sympathy and compassion. Moreover, the genuine altruist desires not just that good is done to others in an inchoate, general sense, but that *they* are author of some of this good. Altruism seems to involve not just some basic social competence, but also a 'metaphysics of agency'; pure altruists want to be the *source* of concrete improvements to others' lives and not just observers of them. We should concede that most of us, much of the time, are only reciprocal altruists: we want the needy to be helped, but we want others to do their share of the helping too (Miller 1989: 113). But whatever sort of altruists we are, we encounter the problem that in contemporary societies (in contrast with those Mauss and Malinowski studied) we do not have much social contact with many of those whose lives most need improvement. Into this gap, between altruists and their beneficiaries are a huge range of charitable and philanthropic organizations as well, of course, as the official welfare agencies of the state. We shall consider the latter shortly. Charities, like official welfare agencies, help meet countless people's urgent, pressing needs; but perhaps more than the latter, they are staffed by people who are committed and passionate; and they help define the altruistic landscape more generally.

The United States has the largest and most developed philanthropic sector in the world. Its citizens are generous donors to a very diverse range of causes, helped in part by the mechanism of payroll giving through which donations are automatically deducted from wages and salaries. America's corporations themselves too have a long and venerable history of philanthropic endeavour. The structure of its famous philanthropic foundations, such as Ford, Carnegie and, more recently, the Bill and Melinda Gates Foundation, date from the early twentieth century (Anheier and Lent 2006). All this altruistic activity occurs alongside and, we would suggest, is partly explained by an equally venerable tradition of fairly paltry and rudimentary welfare provision for its most vulnerable citizens. The UK, though it also has its large-scale philanthropic organizations, such as the Joseph Rowntree Foundation, has experienced a somewhat different trajectory. The great age of philanthropy was the late nineteenth century where a plethora of institutions – foundling hospitals, orphanages, charity schools, settlement houses (bases for outreach social work in the community), societies to help fallen women, societies to help improve the morals of the servant class, and so on – mushroomed into existence, providing, as they did, 'an exemplary outlet for the moral energies and anxieties of highly educated middle class reformers' (Ryan 1996: 76). The Charity Organization Society (COS) was founded in 1869 to assess social need, organize the efforts of charitable institutions, and help them spend their money wisely (for example, avoiding duplication of efforts) (Ryan 1996: 92–3). Today we would see much of the work of the COS embedded within the welfare state: a set of institutions to which we have no choice but to give. But notwithstanding that, giving time, money and other gifts, is something huge numbers of citizens continue to do. Research on philanthropic activity has found it closely correlated with income and education: the better off give more to charity (though some studies show evidence that the worse off give a greater proportion of their income (Mansbridge 1990: 260), and the better educated tend to be more willing to volunteer – of course, many individuals fall into both these categories (Ferguson 1993). Older people tend to donate more time and money than younger people (perhaps because they have more of both to give). The other central explanatory variable is religion: religious people tend to give more than the non-religious, but as one might expect they often direct their efforts to religious rather than secular causes. This is particularly true in the United States where more than half of all giving is directed towards religious organizations (Schokkaert and van Ootegem 2000: 93).

   This last fact reminds us of the important truth that charitable endeavour is intimately connected to personal identity and identification; social contexts shaped by social processes tend to lead people of type A to support causes of type B because they regard B as peculiarly valuable (at least for them), in contrast to other causes (O'Connor 1987). This, at least, is how we would explain the phenomenon of charity. The rational agency perspective, by contrast, highlights the choice element in individual giving through the claim that giving a gift is just like buying a good, both are ways of purchasing satisfaction (Davis 1992: 16). Consider, for example, the reasoning of people who donated blood (a phenomenon we shall consider in more detail shortly). This cost them some time, a little pain, and so on. But:

> in return they got a cup of tea, contact with friendly and grateful medical personnel, and an inner reassurance that they had done a good deed, had contributed to the well-being of some unknown unfortunate ... [Therefore] people who donated blood were making a profit, their costs were less than their rewards.
>
> (Davis 1992: 15)

Accepting this view eases the way to a marketized blood system: cash payment for blood is merely a more tangible and concrete kind of profit. As Davis convincingly argues, however, the 'purchase of satisfaction' metaphor is very much a third person description of what occurs in blood donation and other charitable endeavour: it does not capture how agents themselves understand their actions (Davis 1992: 16–22). A woman who donated her savings to help the families of the 116 children who died in the Aberfan disaster in 1966, when a school was hit by a rock slide, wrote 'I was saving it up for a new coat. Oh God, I wish I had save [sic] more' (cited in Davis 1992: 17). 'It is extraordinarily unlikely that this woman thought she was 'purchasing' satisfaction for herself,' he comments: 'she suffered a movement of the spirit; suffered anguish at the sorrow of others; sacrificed her coat and continued to wish she had more to contribute' (Davis 1992: 17). Davis's view is consonant with Sen's account of commitment above: buying a new coat was the way this woman thought she could purchase most welfare, but donating the money was what she thought she ought to do; she had a commitment to helping the bereaved families.

The real critique of charity is a moral one, and it applies whether we accept the rational choice explanation or the more sociological one we've briefly sketched. The critique is that people's decisions to support one cause rather than another do not track genuine social need (De Wispelaere 2004). Consider, for example, the distinction between the deserving and the undeserving poor, a division which had its heyday in the late nineteenth century but which has enjoyed something of a comeback since the

Thatcherite assault on the welfare state in 1980s Britain. Supporting the distinction are the values of individual freedom and
personal responsibility, and the moral institution of blame. Con-
testing it is the contention that the personal characters of the
unworthy poor are predictably encouraged (if not caused) by the
social conditions in which they find themselves: low wage,
mindless jobs often co-existing with the meaninglessness of mass
unemployment, poor housing, hierarchically organized social
structures, and so on (Ryan 1996: 91). Anyone who takes the
latter view may consider the efforts of those concerned only to
assist the deserving poor to be less than fully philanthropic.

'[A] society without private philanthropy,' writes one moral
philosopher, 'would be a morally impoverished society because it
would lack the elements of spontaneous generosity and effec-
tively benevolent fellow-feeling that are priceless aspects of
human community' (Gewirth 1987: 78). That may be true, but it
runs up against the fact that charitable endeavour and impartial
justice are not the same thing. Indeed, from a historical perspective, the trend has increasingly been to accommodate the needs of
the poor and vulnerable; to see our duties towards them as a
matter of justice, not charity; and to institutionalize these duties in
progressively larger and more inclusive welfare apparatuses. The
growth of the welfare state in twentieth-century Britain is exemplary in this regard. '[M]oral progress,' argues Buchanan, 'to a
large extent, consists of the expansion of the realm of justice into
what we previously believed to be the domain of charity' (Buchanan 1996: 99). If this is the case, however, it is not clear what
space is left for altruism. The distinctively altruistic virtues of
compassion, beneficence, generosity, sympathy, and so on, would
seem to be left without the social practices in which they could
flourish. Every private charitable institution, if its cause is morally urgent enough, would have its rationale undercut by an
enlarged sphere of state action. In this respect, champions of the
New Right who urge a minimal state, individual freedom and
self-sufficiency have a point. They tend to be enthusiastic sup-
porters of a thriving charitable sector for two related reasons:
first, charitable giving reconciles social need with individual
liberty since it removes the coercion which tax-financed welfare
provision involves – individuals can decide whether to give to
their fellow citizens or not; second, if they do choose to give, this
strengthens the altruistic virtues of compassion, sympathy,

benevolence, and so on, which otherwise tend to get submerged beneath the edifice of large, bureaucratic, welfare states. By delimiting social justice, altruism has space to grow. Moreover, the indigent who must help themselves in the absence of state provision strengthen their own independence and self-reliance: they have no choice but to become deserving poor: '[W]e require some sort of distinction between justice and charity to help us separate what is owed from what may be freely given,' argues one writer and, also, he adds, 'to enliven the virtues' (Den Uyl 1987: 202).

Historically speaking, the distinction between justice and charity is not a stable one. In an interesting essay that traces the evolution of the relationship between the two ideas, Schneewind explains how medieval philosophers were much exercised with the spiritual condition of the poor: if we helped the poor it was to save them from being morally demeaned (Schneewind 1996: 54). This attitude was part and parcel of Christian teaching that we should love our neighbours: we should be concerned for their welfare and endeavour to be selfless ourselves. As we saw in Chapter 1, eighteenth-century moralists like Hutcheson and Hume were also much concerned with our motives as (at least potentially), altruistic, benevolent beings (Schneewind 1996: 63–5). Around the same time, however, as Schneewind explains, the idea began to take hold that the better off had duties to aid and assist their worse off fellows. However, once those duties are institutionalized and financed by taxation, they become part of social justice and have little to do with altruism.

In his study of the 'voluntary impulse', Prochaska urges a 'welfare pluralism' where a flourishing voluntary sector incorporating local decision-making, philanthropy and self-help, would sit happily alongside a government that met citizens' welfare needs while promoting policies to foster local voluntary initiatives (Prochaska 1988: 3). Our question is, notwithstanding the accuracy of this description in practice, whether the basic dichotomy it supposes – between justice and charity – can be defended in theory.[2] One defence, suggested by Gewirth, is for private philanthropy to supplement state-financed welfare by focusing on important though nonetheless not vital areas of human well-being which lie outside the purview of our duties of social justice: intellectual and aesthetic culture, for example (Gewirth 1987: 77). Based on this view, the Joint Council for the

Welfare of Immigrants (JCWI), for example, would be co-opted into the state (since if, in an ideal world, the state really did treat immigrants justly there would be no need for the JCWI to check that it did), while the Council for the Protection of Rural England might remain independent. However, this seems a weak argument. If a good meets a genuine human need such that it would be unjust to deny it to anyone, then its potential recipients will quite legitimately want a guarantee that it will be provided; and only the state with the legal instruments at its command can make such guarantees. It is true that goods which merely satisfied some people's wants – and intellectual and aesthetic culture, for example, tend to be a minority interest – could be met by the voluntary sector, but this would severely limit the scope for charitable altruism. Brody maintains that there is no genuine welfare good which could not in principle be provided by the state (Brody 1987).

The distinction between justice and charity remains nonetheless an intuitively plausible one and, notwithstanding the critical role which institutionalized welfare should have in a civilized society, we see four reasons why the charitable provision of welfare goods should continue to play some part. First, since voluntary sector employees often work closer to the reality of local, social needs than state officials, charity has an important epistemic role in identifying and discovering new needs – those which bureaucracies tend to miss. The state will know which are the pockets of deprivation in a town, but it may be third sector activists on the ground who, for example, first discover the outbreak of tuberculosis. Second, as Brody (1987) suggests (and den Uyl intimates) one role of the state is to encourage altruistic virtues in its citizens, and a crucial way it can do this is by leaving them some space for private philanthropy. In fact it can do more. By making philanthropic activity tax-exempt – as is common in the United States – the state can encourage the virtue of voluntary giving without, self-defeatingly, compelling it. Third and relatedly, widespread charitable and voluntary activity involving relatively well-developed social groups and institutions is an important part of civil society, providing citizens with valuable participation goods and acting as a counterweight to state power. Elderly Jews, for example, may prefer for their day centre to be organized by a Jewish welfare charity rather than the local council. Fourth is the obvious but sometimes forgotten fact that not all charity *can* be institutionalized. Prochaska notes how the 1952 Nathan Committee, charged by Parliament with investigating the nature and extent of charity in Britain, 'uncovered a rich seam of unpublicized neighbourliness and familial kindness' and concluded that such activities made 'satisfactory social relationships possible' (Prochaska 1988: 8). These four points together do not provide a knock down reply to the argument canvassed earlier that if a good is sufficiently important for human well-being then its provision should be guaranteed, necessarily invoking legal sanction. But they place the argument in the context of a more complex social reality and surround it with countervailing moral considerations. They strongly suggest that, notwithstanding the charity/justice division, some space should be negotiated for avenues of altruistic expression in contemporary societies. We shall return to this issue in the final chapter.

The Gift Relationship

One writer who has a rather different view of the relationship between altruism and justice is Richard Titmuss in his classic of social policy, *The Gift Relationship* ([1970] 1997). Titmuss, Professor of Social Administration at the London School of Economics, already had an international reputation as a scholar of social policy before *The Gift Relationship* – the culmination of his life's work – was published in 1970. Like all of Titmuss's work, it must be placed in the context of the rise of the post-Second World War welfare state and his engagement with it. Welfare in Britain, of course, pre-dates that war and, in fact, has a long history. The first poor law which levied compulsory local rates to assist the indigent was enacted in 1572; philanthropic endeavour was as we saw a pastime of the Victorian middle classes; and the reforming Liberal Government of 1906–14 introduced limited educational, housing and pension provision, as a way of bolstering Britain's status as a major economic power and pre-empting working class support for the newly emergent Labour Party (Page 1996: 17–59). The Second World War, however, was a turning point because it inflicted indiscriminate hardship. It visited a common experience of suffering on all social groups, cutting across divisions of wealth and class, and in the immediate post-war period demands for universal, non-selective, unconditional, egalitarian social benefits became more clamorous (Titmuss 1950; Dryzek and Goodin

1986; Page 1996: 60–94). This found political expression in the election of the 1945 Labour Government. Titmuss's hope was that the welfare state it augmented so dramatically could institutional-ize something of the early twentieth-century working class friendly (i.e. mutual assurance) societies, while retaining much of their ethos and communal spirit (Jordan 1989: 79–80). *The Gift Relationship's* topic – a defence of voluntary blood donation – needs therefore to be embedded within Titmuss's more general socialist-communitarian argument for the welfare state.

In 1968, the right-wing think tank, the Institute for Economic Affairs (IEA), had published a pamphlet entitled *The Price of Blood*, which had argued for the introduction of a fee-paying system in blood donation (IEA 1968). Remunerating donors with a fee, the IEA argued, would encourage more to come forward, help retain those who had already donated and better enable medical authorities to match demand with supply of blood, thus reducing wastage and promoting efficiency. Blood could and should be treated as a commodity like any other economic good. Titmuss aimed to counter this view. The commodification of blood, he feared, could lead to the marketization of every other welfare good – medicine, education, social security, foster care, and so on.

> All policy would become in the end economic policy and the only values that would count would be those that could be measured in terms of money and pursued in the dialectic of hedonism … To abolish the moral choice of giving to strangers could lead to an ideology to end all ideologies.
>
> (Titmuss [1970] 1997: 58)

Although, as this quotation suggests, Titmuss's primary aim was to argue for the moral superiority of voluntary blood dona-tion, he also believed that a non-marketized donor system was more economically efficient than a fee-based one. This conclu-sion was reached on the basis of a large-scale survey of donations in the UK which was compared with the available data in the US. There, blood donation was becoming increasingly subject to the laws of the market throughout the 1960s. 'Responsibility fee' donors donated in order to avoid being charged a fee for blood they or a family member had earlier received. 'Family credit' donors gave blood as a kind of insurance premium: in return for their donation they and their family's blood needs would be guaranteed to be met for the year. These two types accounted for about half of all US donors. Both these groups were disproportionately comprised of poorer citizens and their motivation to donate – given the exchange relations involved – was primarily economic; neither were instances of spontaneous altruism (Titmuss [1970] 1997: 136). A further one-third of all US donations were directly sold in the free market to hospitals and commercial blood banks, usually in large cities. Most of these donors belonged to the most vulnerable sections of society since they were most likely to see their blood fee as a much needed source of cash. Thus a disproportionately high number of paid donors were unemployed, on low incomes, unskilled and/or black. Moreover, a high proportion of this underclass, were (as described to Titmuss) 'dope addicts, liars, degenerates, unemployed derelicts, prison narcotic users, bums, the faceless, undernourished and unwashed, junkies, hustlers and ooze-for-booze donors' (168–9). In the United States of the 1960s a new class was emerging, concluded Titmuss, of 'an exploited human population of high blood yielders' (172).

Leaving aside for the moment the ethics of this situation, the market in blood emerging in America was, Titmuss maintained, more wasteful and inefficient than a voluntary system. Those who sold their blood tended to be those desperate for money, and were often afflicted with disease, drug addiction, alcoholism or had had recent inoculations, all of which disqualified them as donors. Because blood suppliers did not disclose to medical authorities the source of the blood they sold them – indeed had an interest in not doing so in order not to discourage potential donors – recipients were more likely to receive bad blood (infected with hepatitis, for example) putting their own health at risk. Health authorities in a commercialized system then had to bear the administrative cost of discovering whether the blood they received was contaminated. It was in general more bureaucratic than a voluntary system and hence, per unit of blood supplied, it was more expensive to run. Titmuss estimated blood in the US was 5 to 15 times more expensive to collect, than in the UK. Moreover, suppliers of blood to recipients had to bear the litigation costs which bad blood would entail.

These arguments have not, according to one commentator otherwise sympathetic to Titmuss, stood the test of time (Le Grand 1997: 334). The administrative efficiency of Britain's voluntary, compared to the United States's commercial system, may have been due simply to the particular way the two systems were arranged at the time. Certainly from a theoretical point of view, one would expect a market-based blood system to be able to match supply and demand, avoid shortages and surpluses, and cut unnecessary bureaucratic costs (Arrow 1972). However, while Titmuss's economic arguments may be dated, they are not the main plank of his objections to a commercialized blood system. The reason why *The Gift Relationship* is still read and discussed is the powerful moral case Titmuss makes in favour of voluntary blood donation.

For Titmuss, blood donation was peculiarly altruistic because there was scarcely any tangible reward for giving (a cup of tea and a biscuit), no penalty for not giving, and above all, because it was a symbolic gift of life to an unnamed stranger (Titmuss [1970] 1997: 127–8, 140). The choice to give blood is an act of 'creative altruism' through which one expresses one's trust that strangers would give one the same gift in return should the need arise (279, 307). Most altruism, by contrast, takes place between people with some prior social connection: mother and child, lord and serf, immigrant and fellow national, and so on. A donor's blood, by contrast, may find itself circulating around the body of someone of a quite different age, gender, job, income group, social class and religion. This made it a particularly valuable gift. Blood was not merely symbolically important as something vital for human life, its status as a donated gift released in human beings their most altruistic, communitarian motives and served to bind together a society of strangers marked by market-generated inequalities and other social divisions. The internalized duty of blood donors – that one ought to help one's fellow citizens – could be generalized to provide a moral foundation for the welfare state as a whole.

Titmuss's survey, carried out with the National Blood Transfusion Service revealed that donors, categorised by age, sex, marital status, earnings and social class, were roughly representative of the population as a whole, lending support to his thesis that blood donation was an altruistic gift to strangers. On the other hand, when donors were asked what first motivated them to give blood, they responded with many different kinds of answers, revealing a variety of different sorts of motivations (Titmuss [1970] 1997: 293–302). About 10 per cent of donors, for example, reported motives of reciprocity. They believed either that they ought to repay the gift of blood donated to them or a family member, or they anticipated that they or a family member might one day need blood and wanted to create some moral credit. A further 30 per cent had responded to an appeal by their family, friends or in the media; their answers are harder to classify since being asked by someone else cannot itself be a motive. (One respondent said she had been coerced by her husband (300).) Others gave in gratitude for their own good health (1.4 per cent); out of a sense of duty (3.5 per cent); because they were aware there was a need for blood (6.4 per cent); or because they were continuing a habit first started during the Second World War (11.7 per cent); among other answers. Again, all of these may, but need not, be consistent with altruistic motivations. Notwithstanding these definitional problems, Titmuss classified 26.4 per cent of donors as altruists. 'Knowing I mite be saving somebody life,' wrote one. 'I felt it was a small contribution I could make to the welfare of humanity,' said another (Titmuss [1970] 1997: 293). However, when some of the other motives above were also included, especially duty, awareness of blood shortages, response to appeals and reciprocity – on an interpretation of reciprocity as trust that others will do likewise – over 80 per cent of donors could be classed as altruists in the broader sense of having a high sense of social responsibility towards the needs of other members of their society (302–3). They had the sorts of motives which citizens ought to have in a modern welfarist society.

The Gift Relationship resonates with a powerful moral force and no one reading it can avoid being touched, if not persuaded, by its arguments. Titmuss himself, however, does not always distinguish between them as clearly as he might do. But, besides his probably erroneous view that a market for blood was economically inefficient, three moral arguments for non-marketized, voluntary donation can be identified (Le Grand 1997: 333–4). First, then, Titmuss believes that a commercialized blood system was socially unjust. As could be seen in the United States, it exploited poorer, more vulnerable members of society because it distributed a vital resource away from them and towards better off people less likely to be donors themselves. This argument needs to be analysed with care, however. After all, a blood seller, unlike a blood donor, receives money in return, an equally vital resource. Moreover, they make up the blood they have donated in a short space of time, enabling them to sell again. Selling blood is a genuinely free choice since there is no special penalty attached to forbearance – unlike, say, workers forced to accept starvation wages. Thus while a society where an underclass services the blood needs of the better off hardly seems morally admirable, it is hard to identify the sense in which it is exploitative or unjust.

Titmuss's second argument, by contrast, is more promising. Since 'the opportunity to behave altruistically … is an essential human right,' he writes, 'this book is about the definition of freedom' (Titmuss [1970] 1997: 59). The choice between monetized and non-monetized systems for the collection of blood is, in essence, a question of freedom. 'Should men be free to sell their blood?' he asks. 'Or should this freedom be curtailed to allow them to give or not give blood?' (59), Titmuss's argument is that the ostensibly free market actually eclipses the freedom of people to give their blood. '[P]olicy,' he writes, 'should enable men to give to unnamed strangers. They should not be coerced or constrained by the market' (310). But on the face of it, this argument makes no sense. The marketization of blood would surely enhance freedom: it would give people the new freedom to sell their blood, while at the same time retaining their old freedom to donate it (Arrow 1972: 349–50). If the market gives people the choice between giving and selling: it can hardly be said to coerce or constrain. Titmuss's point, however, is more subtle. The marketization of blood would erode people's altruistic motivation to donate. Since many people would be bound to sell their blood if enabled to do so, few people would choose to give theirs when they saw others selling. The freedom to give to an unnamed stranger is a more valuable freedom – an act of 'creative altruism' which helps integrate the wider community – than the freedom to sell. Since the market would drive out altruistic motivations, it would diminish freedom in this evaluative sense. As Singer has put it, '[t]he decision not to interfere [in the market] affects individual choices just as much as the decision to interfere does' (Singer 1977: 164; see also Singer 1973). This argument is more plausible, but it has still been contested by several writers. To begin with, as the economist Kenneth Arrow complains, Titmuss's prediction is not supported by any empirical evidence or theorctical analysis (Arrow 1972: 350–1). Why should a market for blood diminish the use of the more valuable freedom to give?

Second, as one contemporary libertarian writer has pointed out, if a market for blood exists alongside a donor system then participants in the latter can more easily demonstrate their charity, generosity and compassion than if it did not (Machan 1997: 252–3). The altruistic virtues flower more beautifully in the soil of hard-nosed economic realism. And indeed there are goods both sold in the market and freely given where it is the latter, non-marketized version which is more valued by society: sex is perhaps the best example (Lomasky 1983).

Notwithstanding his references to it, Titmuss's basic case against a market in blood has little to do with freedom. His central argument, to which the former three are merely preludes, is that the marketization of blood would morally impoverish the relations between fellow citizens (Archard 2002). Blood – realistically and symbolically – helps constitute life. Its voluntary, uncoerced, unrewarded exchange among a group of people who are, strictly speaking, strangers to one another, helps bind them together as a civilized human community, one that exemplifies the communitarian virtues of solidarity, fellowship, and so on (Page 1996: 94–102). It is no surprise that a Canadian study, conducted a few years after Titmuss's research, found that people who felt least integrated into their local community were those least likely to donate blood; while conversely regular donors had the strongest communal commitments (Lightman 1981). Just as the circulation of blood around the person feeds the organs and enables them to work as part of a single body, so its circulation around a society helps constitute it as a society and enables its members to enjoy social relationships of moral quality with their fellow citizens. This may seem, of course, an exaggeration. After all, only about 4 per cent of the population are blood donors. But Titmuss turns this point around. He argues that the decline of formalized systems of gift exchange in modern societies has made more valuable those few avenues citizens have for the expression of altruism (Titmuss 1997: 290–1), even if, we might add, not all of them make use of it. More importantly, he also places blood donation in the context of his general socialist-communitarian argument for the welfare state. This is never quite stated explicitly by Titmuss in *The Gift Relationship*, but it comes across clearly to anyone reading it and it is consistent with his other writings. Thus in his 1968 *Commitment to Welfare*, for example, Titmuss argued that the purpose of the welfare state was to raise citizens' dignity and promote their freedom, equality and social integration. Private charity, by contrast, tends to perpetuate discrimination and stigma, and when combined with selective, in other words, non-universal welfare provision visits on welfare recipients a 'humiliating loss of status, dignity and self-respect' (Titmuss 1968: 129).

At root, therefore, *The Gift Relationship* is about the moral value of two visions of society. On the one hand, there is an atomistic market society, enabling (value-neutral) freedom and choice, and liberating individuals from fetters on their accumulation of private wealth. This is Titmuss's 'ideology to end all ideologies'. On the other, there is a socialist-communitarian society in which social policy does not simply meet citizens' needs, but is directed more generally towards the fulfilment of moral goals: community, dignity, equality and universality. It is true that blood could be bought and sold in a society where citizens' welfare needs were still met by universal provision, free at the point of dispensation (for example, the NHS could be the sole purchaser for citizens' blood which it could dispense for no other fee than general taxation).[3] But Titmuss fears this might have a domino effect. If blood donation was commercialized and blood treated as a commodity, then every other welfare good might be too (Titmuss [1970] 1997: 263). In his defence of Titmuss, Singer mentions the 'experimental evidence for the view that altruism fosters increased altruism' (Singer 1972: 319). We reviewed some of this evidence in the last chapter. Instead of the domino effect, we should have, in Titmuss's view, a virtuous circle of altruism. Experience of others' giving would encourage citizens to give themselves; and as they met others' needs and had their own needs met in turn, citizens would increasingly think of themselves as active members of a common moral community.

These lofty sentiments do not remove the fact that there seems to be a tension, unrecognized by Titmuss, at the heart of *The Gift Relationship*. On the one hand, he interprets blood donation as a pure, free gift, an act of genuinely 'creative altruism', peculiarly altruistic because it is impersonal. '[T]here are no personal, predictable penalties for not giving,' Titmuss notes, 'no socially enforced sanctions of remorse, shame or guilt' ([1970] 1997: 74). On the other hand, he construes blood donation as an exchange relationship which fosters social integration. He expresses, for example, the Maussian sentiment, that '[t]o give is to receive – to compel some return or create some obligation' (277). When positive moral obligations enjoy widespread recognition in society they tend, Titmuss hopes, to promote a sense of community. A gift, however, is not the same thing as an exchange (Harris 1987: 70–2). Titmuss wants to stress that blood is a gift because of his hostility towards free marketeers who argue that payment for blood would simply augment the psychic return that donors can't but receive, as well as promote economic efficiency. Blood is humanity: it is beyond the capitalist cash nexus. But in order to sustain his communitarian argument for the welfare state as a scheme of generalized reciprocity, Titmuss must say that donors have a moral entitlement to, and a social expectation of, a return 'gift'. The problem is that market and community, despite the fundamental differences between them, both have at their core the critical notion of exchange. Perhaps the reason why the crucial gift/exchange distinction is overlooked is because of the anonymity of blood donation. A favour I do for a friend is most of all a gift. There may be some thought of reciprocal entitlement in my mind, but if I'm in need and genuinely not disappointed by my friend's reluctance, it looks like I've been fairly altruistic. Now relations between citizens have in common with relations between friends a variety of transactions of exchange; these are, if you like, the modalities of the relationship and give it its character and substance. But the impersonality of blood donation, together with the fact that donors rarely know if and when they will need blood themselves, serve to make it hard to tell whether donors' blood is perceived by them to be a gift or an exchange. As we saw, when Titmuss asked them, donors reported a variety of motives, not always easy to classify on the altruism–reciprocity–exchange continuum (Page 1996: 98–100).

Altruism, welfare and duty

Ideas of reciprocity and exchange seem a promising foundation for the welfare state, and we shall consider them in the next chapter. But whether altruism is of much help in justifying state welfare is a separate and more controversial question. Approving references to Mauss appear throughout Titmuss's book, but in fact Mauss's argument for the welfare state at the end of *The Gift* –

where the mass of evidence from his wide-ranging anthropological survey is put to commendatory use – has little to do to with altruism (Mauss [1950] 2002: 86–105). Just as Trobriand Islanders enjoyed complex gift/return gift social relations, so, according to Mauss, different social classes in post-war France had reciprocal obligations to one another. In particular, the wealth produced by the working class that was their 'gift' to society as they received a disproportionately small part of the proceeds. This, according to Mauss, obliged their better off fellows to reciprocate with return gifts of unemployment benefit, sick pay, pensions, and so on. Society would progress only if socially embedded practices of giving and receiving were stabilized. Workers should not demand too much, Mauss implies, but neither should their middle class beneficiaries undervalue the workers' contribution in estimating the return gifts they owed. 'Give as much as you take', says the Maori proverb which Mauss cites approvingly, and 'all shall be very well' (Mauss [1950] 2002: 91).

We need to consider, however, people who give anyway, regardless of how much, if anything, they take or can expect to take. The genuine altruist, we want to suggest, is someone who is free, in some sense, to be non-altruistic; that they have chosen to take the more charitable path is what makes their altruism genuine. If too many citizens' non-altruism expresses itself in their reluctance to meet the welfare needs of their vulnerable fellows, the state, taking some responsibility for the latters' needs, may decide to institutionalize the provision of welfare goods. In a society of any size this will be done through taxation, with welfare itself being delivered by trained professionals. Tax, however, by its nature, is something one is not free not to pay. And if taxpayers lack that freedom, then, qua the provision of welfare goods to their fellow citizens, we can hardly consider them altruists (Harris 1987: 65; Seglow 2004).

Plainly there is no dilemma here if people would (hypothetically) have chosen to do what they have a legal duty to do. But this is not the way people generally think about altruism. Altruism, we believe, centrally involves a person's motive to help another; the altruist is responding to the need or vulnerability of their beneficiary. The altruist and their beneficiary have a direct relationship, one which is not mediated or structured by external moral concerns about what the altruist should do. This we believe is what Titmuss meant when he said that blood donation belongs to the sphere of 'ultra-obligations' ([1970] 1997: 279); and it is also consonant with Jordan's point that altruism can involve expanding one's sympathies beyond one's current social roles (as when I give first aid to a stranger, for example) (Jordan 1989: 169). This view may seem hard to square with the idea that social roles define much everyday altruism; between parent and child, for example, or between villagers in the kind of nineteenth-century Russian commune romanticized by Kropotkin in his *Mutual Aid* ([1910] 1987). In the latter case, we would suggest that what is involved is less pure gift than an exchange. Villagers helped each other, each in the expectation that they would be helped in turn. But whether altruism involves return gifts or not, the more a person is merely fulfilling the demands of their social role, the less their behaviour is altruistic. A parent who looks after their child because they think that that is what parents ought to do is less altruistic than one who does so because they recognize their child's neediness. No doubt most parents act from both these sorts of motives. But citizens in contemporary anonymous societies meet each other's needs largely through impersonal, legal channels that prescribe for them fairly settled institutional roles. They lack the discretion which altruism entails. When I look in on the old person next door I am being altruistic, playing the role of a good neighbour, but I am also creating that role, and it is in that creative aspect that my altruism lies. When my taxes fund their pension I am not being altruistic, or hardly so.

We earlier identified altruism with creativity within, and action beyond, social roles. It is in these spaces, we believe, where most altruism occurs. Citizenship, being legally defined, is a fairly tightly scripted social role. No doubt some citizens (and perhaps all of them at least some of the time) identify the plight of the old, the young, the sick and the unemployed in their society with the taxes the state levies so to finance caring for them, but the connection is a rather contingent one. Through wholehearted giving we demonstrate that 'no man is an island', and practically refute the rational economic view of individuals. When giving is regularized and institutionalized, however morally laudable that may be, just a little bit of the island mentality is re-introduced.

Notes

1 Serge-Christophe Kolm relates how, during his first visit to Africa, he was given a chicken by a villager, a gift which, though not needed, he did not feel he could refuse. His guide suggested a return gift would be appropriate. 'As I remarked that

I had nothing I could dispense with (I needed my shirt and my camera was much too expensive to be given), it was suggested that the return gift could be money and that, incidentally, the market price of a chicken could be a suitable amount' (Kolm 2000a: 14–5).

2   It's worth noting that utilitarianism finds it hard to draw a line between justice and charity (Ryan 1996: 77); but since there is an intuitive line to be drawn this can only count as a weakness of utilitarianism.

3   Harris has suggested such a scheme for the kidneys. See John Harris (2003) 'Gifting organs is no different from their sale, *The Guardian*, 5 December.

6

Altruism: fundamental for a human future

Our journey into altruism has led us to explore a variety of disciplines: moral philosophy, evolutionary biology, social psychology, economics and political science among them. Altruism is a phenomenon enmeshed in different spheres of human conduct. Yet these disciplines have strikingly different perspectives: not only do they have different foci and areas of concern, each of them tends to treat, as common sense, conclusions which other disciplines regard as highly controversial; and conversely each questions assumptions which others treat as mundane. For example, economics and evolutionary biology tend to see human beings as essentially amoral creatures, unconcerned with others' interests; social psychology does not consider that altruistic motivations might have evolved at a species level; while political science concentrates almost exclusively on historical and cultural explanations for people's altruistic outlook. Admittedly, it is hardly surprising that different academic disciplines inhabit different intellectual universes. But making use of all of these diverse approaches to get a grasp on a single phenomenon is a bit like asking a number of people for directions to the same destination only to receive a succession of quite different answers.

In this final chapter we again take up three issues which we have already discussed in this book, but this time with a more explicit focus on how other perspectives challenge and question the accounts one approach gives. These three issues are the good of altruism, as seen from an evolutionary perspective; the discretion which altruism seems to involve versus the impartial demands of morality; and the selfishness of market societies compared to the more communal ethos of altruistic ones. We conclude by outlining a unified altruistic perspective on ethics and social life, one which integrates reason and emotion, and which is (or so we argue) fundamental for a genuinely human future.

As we saw in Chapter 3, the difficulty in relying upon evolutionary biology to give an account of altruism is that its preoccupation with explaining what appears to be a counter-evolutionary strategy, leaves little room for the genuinely moral aspects of the phenomenon. The meta-narrative of the struggle for survival has selfishness at its core. A number of theorists who cleave to evolutionary assumptions have, however, sought to explain aspects of moral behaviour within their framework, and in doing so they have carved a space for altruism and related phenomena. The anthropologist Christopher Boehm (2000), for example, has examined how evolutionary changes might have brought about proto-moral behaviours in ape societies and early human communities. There are good evolutionary reasons for a group to suppress sexual behaviour that is likely to cause conflict within it, and more generally to regulate the behaviour of those who are deviant. Bonobo chimpanzee communities controlled their members deviant behaviour, and the way they acted when food was distributed, in political ways. Further evidence for proto-moral behaviour in primates comes from work carried out on Rhesus monkeys and studies of chimpanzees. In Rhesus monkeys, Frans de Waal reports punishment and reconciliation behaviour that is controlled in such a way that it reasserts rather than undermines group unity. Punishment is visited in a more reparative way, achieving social inclusion not its opposite (de Waal 1996: 104). Food distribution can be an occasion for monkeys to achieve political ends, such as status and popularity. Specifically, in de Waal's study at Arnhem Zoo, monkeys who went without their share to benefit others were seen as generous, augmenting their status. Later, in human hunter-gatherer societies, Boehm speculates, codes of practice emerged where deviants recognized and regulated themselves: thus an individual who killed another, usually as a result of male sexual or food competition, would exclude 'themselves from the band either permanently or until tempers cool[ed]' (Boehm 2000: 95). This kind of primitive moral norm characterized humans in the late paleolithic era. In other situations, the solution is provided by the group itself, which enforces a code of practice to control conflicts. Because this code applied to every member of the group equally, Boehm regards it as egalitarian. Such groups were also marked by more overtly political behaviour including the formation of coalitions, the desire for domination, and the dislike of subordination. Fully formed moral communities were not able to develop until abstract communication had emerged. With this in place, members were able to influence one another's behaviour in order to sustain a fairly sophisticated conception of social order. Boehm (2000) suggests that this involved a degree of personal autonomy and equality, in place of hierarchy and dominance, and members were able to reflect on the nature of their social life. Along similar lines, Eliot Sober and David Sloan Wilson (1998) in their work on the evolution of altruism, suggest that the emergence of rational thought provided humans with the ability to bring about phenotypical changes in human beings (changes in their observable characteristics), including the adoption of moral norms. For altruism, as one kind of norm, to be a successful strategy in social and cultural evolution, beliefs about behaviours that are conducive to the promotion of social functioning must have developed in a non-adaptive way. Such beliefs and behavioural practices are conducive to a certain kind of cultural ethos (a more altruistic one), but not identifiably biologically relevant or strategies that achieve biological success. Altruistic acts that are considered to be kind and promote some notion of goodness, such as community spirit, are not likely to have much to do with genetic evolution.

While altruism may have had its origins in a genetic strategy, when humans held certain beliefs about the significance of unselfish behaviour and acted upon them, it has become something different. Anthony O'Hear reinforces this when he points out the limits of a purely biological account:

> Precisely because we are self conscious and reflective agents, group selection can never be a sufficient condition for the presence in society or culture of particular sets of beliefs or practices ... Individuals in that society have to be convinced or forced to adopt the beliefs or practices.
>
> (O'Hear 1997: 155)

In other words, humans (being what they are), group selection and the struggle for survival, can never be the sole explanation for the presence in society of a belief or practice, altruistic or otherwise. A credible explanation must also account for the distinctive capacities of communication and deliberation, and our ability reflectively to endorse or reject certain modes of behaviour. Along these lines, Michael Ruse has suggested that rather than humans entering into the world with a blank slate, we have innate capacities and dispositions for culture to work upon in our moral development (Ruse 1991). He speculates that it is these innate dispositions which lead us towards biological altruism, in other words the kind of helping behaviour that the purely evolutionary account seeks to explain. The content of these dispositions is our belief that we should behave in ways that are helpful and caring towards our fellow humans (notwithstanding the contrary dispositions that humans also exhibit). Just because the purely evolutionary account suggests that we have selfish genes, to use Richard Dawkins' terminology, this does not mean that we are always selfish. On Ruse's account, it is not altruism alone which is a good strategy for organisms, such as humans' long-term evolutionary success, but rather our beliefs about the moral goodness of altruism. 'We are moral,' he says, 'because our genes as fashioned by natural selection fill us with thoughts about being moral' (Ruse 1991: 504). More strongly: 'our moral beliefs are simply an adaptation put in place by natural selection in order to further our reproductive ends ... Morality is no more than a collective illusion fobbed off on us by our genes for reproductive ends' (Ruse 1991: 506).

Interesting as Ruse's position is, his argument still cannot tell us why it is good to be altruistic. In this respect, his account suffers from the same deficiency as the evolutionary explanations we encountered in Chapter 3. Such explanations tend to make mistakes when they seek to explain altruism as a moral phenomenon, assuming, for example, that evolution somehow can generate ethical values or that Social Darwinism is itself a kind of proto-morality. Indeed, it would seem that evolutionary altruism is quite unrelated to moral altruism. For what even the more sophisticated versions of the evolutionary paradigm cannot account for is how morality could evolve and, once evolved what explains its normative power? For this the moral argument is required.

While Ruse has turned to Kant, Hume and Aristotle's moral philosophies, to see if they might be grafted on to an evolutionary argument, Oldenquist maintains that utilitarianism is the place to find a connection between the two paradigms (Oldenquist 1990). Oldenquist's overall aim is to provide, what he calls, a bridge theory which will provide an explanation of morality's normative potency in terms conducive to evolutionary biology (Oldenquist 1990: 123–7). Such a bridge theory must take a naturalistic approach to morality: instead of assuming that moral values are somehow 'out there', inscribed in the universe, naturalism seeks to infer them from the invariant form of human social living. Christopher Boehm's anthropological suggestions about the codification of kinds of behaviours that deal with deviance, avoiding the conflict it can bring to a group, would be an example of the starting point of a naturalistic account. Oldenquist's argument is that if morality is conceived of in rule-utilitarian terms then there need be no conflict between it and evolutionary biology. Normatively speaking, rule-utilitarianism is the theory that society should adopt those moral rules or practices which, if adhered to will produce the most utility (more than other sets of rules or no rules at all). Thus, it is similar to the theory of natural selection, which says that traits will emerge and sustain themselves if they are useful. Putting these two viewpoints together, Oldenquist maintains that human societies will adopt those values that will best contribute to their ongoing survival. This naturalistic mode of argument stands in sharp contrast with moral philosophies which emphasize duties or virtues regardless of their consequences, and hence regardless of their effects on species survival.

Although this conclusion is attractive, it would mean that altruism persists only because it is useful for society and for individuals to flourish, and no more. If it were no longer useful, altruism as a moral phenomenon would cease. Altruism as a mode of behaviour could not be evaluated or judged independent of its function in promoting species survival. In this way, Oldenquist's utilitarian argument is no different from evolutionary ones that take no account of morality whatsoever. It is unable to explain the non-contextual features of altruism, such as the idea that we have obligations of beneficence to strangers. Much of the moral appeal of altruism is lost once it is put exclusively in the service of social utility.

It is not just moral philosophers and evolutionary biologists who have cleaved to Darwinian suppositions about the usefulness of altruistic behaviour. The same assumptions have permeated empirical investigations in the social sciences, with some unfortunate normative implications. A good example is the controversial thesis proposed by Frank Salter in his *Welfare, Ethnicity and Altruism* (Salter 2004: 3–24, 306–27). Salter draws on the Ethnic Nepotism Theory developed by van den Berghe (1981) according to which ethnically similar individuals, because they share a certain proportion of their genes, will engage in nepotistic behaviour in order to perpetuate their own kind. According to Salter, ethnic groups develop solidary relations when they come to think of themselves as families. In order to overcome the free rider problem that altruism so often involves, individuals have an interest in forming trust relationships with others. In seeking to build such relationships, it is natural to look to members of one's own ethnic group, who consequently come to be an extended (if metaphorical) family. Members of one's own ethnic 'family' will be less likely to default on the altruistic obligations they owe to you. By the same token, members of ethnic 'families' who benefit from each other's giving will be reluctant to distribute goods to extra-familial outsiders. Salter's argument, then, is that welfare spending will be higher in ethnically homogenous societies where citizens can regard each other as an extended ethnic family, and lower in more ethnically plural societies. As Walzer has noted in the American context, when politicians urge more generous welfare spending they are likely to claim that all Americans constitute one big family (Walzer 1992). Indeed, Salter's ethnic homogeneity argument is not just a speculative thesis. For not only were welfare rights first entrenched in states which were at the time more ethnically homogenous – Sweden, France and Germany, for example – but higher welfare spending today is positively correlated with the degree of ethnic homogeneity found in a society. Salter does not claim that ethnic homogeneity is the only explanation for the size of the welfare state and public spending. Factors such as ideological tradition and trade union strength are also significant. But the degree of ethnic diversity is, nonetheless, an important part of the explanation of a state's welfare generosity. In general, he concludes, '[p]ublic altruism declines ... when fellow citizens are perceived to belong to different ethnic groups' (Salter 2004: 3).

There is much we can say in reply to the ethnic homogeneity argument. For one thing, there are ethnically diverse states with fairly high welfare spending (France and the Netherlands, for example) and ethnically homogenous states with little tradition of public welfare (such as Singapore or South Korea). For another, it is not at all clear that ethnic groups (all of them?) do regard themselves as extended families: that assumption calls for anthropological investigation. But the most striking thing about the argument is its seeming assumption that welfare altruism is simply a useful convention adopted by members of ethnic groups for their mutual benefit. The argument seems to conflate the empirical and the normative. The idea that public welfare has moral grounds independent of contingent social facts is absent. Those grounds, such as need, right or entitlement are, after all, universal ones which reach across ethnic boundaries. It may be that much altruism occurs within and not between ethnic groups, but welfare is delivered for quite different sorts of reasons.

Salter's homogeneity thesis claims that social heterogeneity erodes both welfare and altruism with which it is identified. But, as we argued in Chapter 5, it is not clear that the idea of welfare has much to do with altruism. One way of forging a connection between the two ideas, however, is to argue that the welfare state is essentially a communitarian institution, a suggestion that is worth exploring a little further. Based on this view, the welfare state is something like Kropotkin's mutual aid in the village writ large. Citizens strongly identify with each other's needs, and the well-being of each member of society is a matter of common concern. Each person believes that their own life is diminished if another's life deteriorates. Goodin maintains that the village society welfare state analogy is a strained one since the latter is a far more impersonal institution in which members 'contract out' meeting each other's welfare needs to professional agencies (Goodin 1988: 113–8). This may be too stark a conclusion, however. The communitarian defence of welfare provision need only maintain that there is such a thing as a communitarian ethos, exhibited, albeit in quite different ways in the nineteenth-century Russian village and the twenty-first-century social democratic state. Elsewhere Goodin, together with Dryzek, has argued that one important explanation for the growth of the post-war British welfare state was the democratization of risk that the war visited upon Britons – the welfare state being an institution that pools risk (Dryzek and Goodin 1986).

In fact, the communitarian argument comes in two different versions which it is important to disentangle. Based on one version, individuals give because it would not occur to them to do anything else. Indeed, if identification with society is sufficiently strong, they may hardly perceive it as a burden. On this view, people's social roles will almost entirely delineate their social obligations. There may be some space left for what Titmuss calls creative altruism but it will be small. We can call this the pure communitarian argument and it seems to resemble most closely the Russian village society that Kropotkin enthusiastically described. The other version is still communitarian but there is not quite the strong identification with others' needs. In this mixed communitarian view, community needs supplementing with another source of norms. These come from the idea of reciprocity. Welfare institutions constitute a system of generalized reciprocity where individuals make sacrifices in the expectation that others will do likewise, when they are in need. Now reciprocity arguments are vulnerable to the free rider dilemma: what assurance do I have in making a sacrifice myself that others will do the same for me when I am in need, especially when, as in generalized reciprocity, it is highly unlikely that the person I call on for help will be the same person that I myself helped? The communitarian part of the argument provides a way out of the dilemma. Communitarian societies have a solidaristic ethos which besides being the source of social integration, also under-writes the trust and mutual assurance necessary to overcome the free rider problem. Because citizens identify with one another, they are willing to suffer the burden of contributing to the social pot – in the knowledge that it is there for them when they need to call upon it.

The mixed communitarian argument has more credibility when both views are put in the context of a market ethos threatening to welfare. The market-erodes-welfare argument points to the spread of market values and virtues, such as individualism, personal liberty, responsibility for self and the accumulation of wealth, all of them antithetical to welfarism (Jordan 1989; Ware 1990). When these take root it becomes psychologically difficult to maintain the more altruistic, welfare-friendly dispositions. A single person cannot be a calculating market agent and a keen-to-do-good altruist. At the same time, proponents of the argument point to certain social trends in market societies, such as increased geographical mobility, and the growth of more impersonal market over more solidaristic non-market transactions. These also erode the motivations on which the welfare state is founded.

The pure communitarian view is highly susceptible to the growth of a market ethos. What occurs here is simply the demise of one kind of society and its replacement with another. There is only so much social space, as it were, for an ideology to occupy, and once the market has replaced community there is no going back. The pure communitarian defence of welfare, however, is not that plausible in the first place. It seems unlikely that many people today would part with their taxes with no concern at all for their own chances of receiving anything in return. In this respect, Goodin's objection that communitarianism trades on a strained analogy between the village and the impersonal, bureaucratic state is correct. The former, of course, delivered welfare in kind, not tax-financed impersonal welfare. But there remains the mixed communitarian view. This offers not only a more realistic account of the way welfare institutions are created and maintained, but it is also less susceptible to the market erosion argument. This is because the norm of reciprocity which operates in the welfare context is closely related to the notion of exchange which is so central to the market. To be sure, two parties can exchange goods without sharing an ideal of reciprocity, but the point is that a market society in which exchange is widespread can help sediment reciprocal relations between strangers. Individuals can give time, money, labour, goods *and* tax-income in the expectation that they will get something in return. In the case of tax-income, this something is public goods which includes welfare. Psychologically, then, there is less distance than at first appears between market values and welfarist ones: they overlap to the degree that individuals give with some expectation of return (and they would not expect that return unless they gave). Moreover, even purely market, non-welfarist transactions require mutual trust: each side needs the assurance that the other will in fact reciprocate.

This point about reciprocity is important because not only does it support a view of welfarism as a quasi-communitarian, quasi-altruistic notion, it also tells against the often made argument that altruism will decline with the growth of market society. Once again, we can consider the spread of a market ethos from a pure communitarian and a mixed communitarian perspective. In the former case, altruism occupies the spaces between social roles. If

I tend a sick neighbour because that is the sort of thing neighbours do then it is not altruistic; if the expectation is that people only look after sick relatives, then my tending my neighbour looks more altruistic. The question for this view is whether altruistic practices will survive as the obligations constitutive of social roles begin to be eroded with the growth of the market. There is no definitive answer which can be given a priori. It's certainly tempting to maintain that as exchange and reciprocity increasingly permeate social relations, people will begin to ask what they can get in return for their endeavours. Where there is little return, there will be little altruism. However, it's not implausible to think that small-scale altruism, as practised between friends and neighbours and within families, will continue. One could argue that these sorts of social relations are a haven from the harsh discipline of the market, and individuals will welcome the non-market norms they foster and maintain. No doubt there is empirical evidence for both conclusions, although in popular rhetoric the former seems more dominant. That the market leads to selfishness is one of the most common charges made against it. The mixed communitarian account is also compatible with the idea of pure altruistic giving. And again, we cannot say for sure, whether with the spread of the norm of reciprocity, altruism will suffer a demise. Relations of reciprocity can occupy different sorts of social contexts, but there is no reason to think that human beings will ever want all their social relations to be governed by it. The mixed account, however, is more conducive to a different view of altruism where altruistic practices are seen to involve generalized reciprocity. Based on this view of altruism people still want to give, they have goodwill towards those whose welfare they can beneficially affect, but they prefer to receive something in return, though not necessarily from the person to whom they gave. Altruism as generalized reciprocity operates in communities of persons who wish each other well but don't want to feel exploited through their own welfarist acts. Central to it, therefore, is the notion of exchange. Of course, the idea that reciprocal altruists desire some benefit in return may make them seem less than altruistic. Altruism, after all, common-sensically, involves the idea of sacrifice. But it is plausible to think that those who help others for others' sake nonetheless do want something in return (if only recognition), and it seems unduly stipulative to insist that altruism must involve a sacrifice for no gain at all.

Granted then that reciprocal altruism is altruism of some sort, it may seem quite consistent with the market, and we would not therefore necessarily expect altruism as generalized reciprocity to decline with the growth of market relations. Altruism construed this way is just another kind of exchange relation. On the other hand, there is nothing intrinsically altruistic in the notion of reciprocity, it depends entirely on the sentiments of those in reciprocal relations. (Thus one successful strategy in Prisoner's Dilemma games is 'tit-for-tat' where A co-operates if and only if B co-operates, but A does not co-operate when B does not – this is a purely reciprocal strategy.) One might argue, therefore, that the dispositions fostered by the growth of market relations are antithetical even to reciprocal altruism. Again, there is no obvious answer to the fate of altruistic practices in market societies: the question calls for further investigation.

David Miller has provided a communitarian defence of the welfare state, making the assumption that most of us are altruists of a more contingent kind. Most of us, he surmises, want the poor, sick and vulnerable to be helped, but we do not want to do too much of that helping ourselves. We are like the bystanders we encountered in Chapter 4. We feel distress at the child drowning in the pond (or the homeless person begging in the shop doorway), but it would be most convenient if someone else could take care of them. Just like bystanders, we are looking for an excuse not to give. This does not mean that we never will. I might be prepared to do my bit if others do too (we all have to pull on a rope with the drowning person clinging on at the other end), or if there is a chance that I too might suffer a similar misfortune – here we return to Dryzek and Goodin's risk-pooling argument for the origins of the welfare state. But we are not saintly participation altruists who derive intrinsic satisfaction from the very performance of our do-gooding activities. Miller argues that the welfare state extracts the more contingent calculating and reciprocal altruists from their dilemma (Miller 1989: ch.4). By enforcing welfare duties, it gives each person the assurance that the needy are helped, together with the guarantee that others are also doing their bit.

Miller, however, goes on to argue that the welfare state is better founded on rights than on altruism. The reason it is financed by coercively imposed taxation is not to overcome the free rider problem among contingent altruists, but rather to ensure that, altruistic or not, the duties consequent on rights to welfare are actually met (Miller 1989: 100; Page 1996: 102). This is another justification for the welfare state, for on the rights-based view, welfarism has little to do with community or with altruism, it is part of social justice. There is a level of decency below which no one's life should fall. The guarantee made by society to its most vulnerable member is expressed in terms of rights. This, it should be said, is a far more common way to defend welfare measures today, at least among political philosophers. Altruism does not have much of a role since if, taxation is compulsory, people's motives become somewhat immaterial (Seglow 2004). Harris (1987) has suggested that citizens in a tax-financed welfare regime still retain the choice of whether to give altruistically or not. Those on PAYE (Pay as you earn system) might resent the fraction of their income deducted at source each month or they might embrace it willingly. If the latter is true, they can meet their duties altruistically. That may be so, but if we have no choice in the matter then our attitudes are rather beside the point. One might argue that there is a non-negligible difference between a choice of attitudes and a choice of actions, and indeed the limitations to the latter can affect the former. Since deciding to adopt different attitudes will, in this case, make no practical difference, it's plausible to think that the number of thoroughgoing altruists who enthusiastically pay their income tax will be rather small.

An important difference between the rights-based and communitarian arguments for welfare provision, one with important implications for our view of altruism is the partiality we think it permissible for people to show to one another. The rights-based view is a universalist one. If people are to give preferential treatment to their family, friends or compatriots, it must be within a moral framework in which the duties they owe to rights-holders are assuredly performed. The communitarian view, by contrast, is partialistic from the start. Welfare is not only a kind of altruism, it is one that by definition involves partiality. In doing so it taps into evolutionary explanations as to why we favour being altruistic to our relatives, friends, or those we recognize as other altruists (as in green beard altruism). But though such an explanation of our altruistic history may be informative, there is no need to be committed to a notion of altruism that perpetuates such partiality. We should remember the genetic fallacy – a thing is not the same as its origins. To be sure, certain features are definitive of altruism, such as taking another's interests as one's own and being motivated to promote them. But others, in this case the evolutionary assumption that altruism has a genetic rationale in perpetuating one's genes in successive generations, may be discarded. This is easier said than done, however. It is one thing to define a morally reformed altruism, it is another to persuade people that this is the form of altruism they should exhibit. A good example of the failure of the latter, and one that seems to strengthen the ethnic nepotism thesis, is an incident that occurred at the Sheffield Northern General Hospital in July 1998. The family of a deceased white man, who were willing for his organs to be donated to others, stipulated that they had to go to white recipients. As a family, they had a very real attachment to the giver, his gift object, and hence, or so they believed, the gift object's recipient. The Department of Health ruled that it was unacceptable for the Hospital Trust to accept organs with conditions attached, and that in this case the conditions demanded could put the recipient and the donor's family in breach of the 1976 Race Relations Act. The organs in this case were, properly speaking, given to the Hospital Trust to do with as they saw medically fit. An editorial in the medical journal, the *Lancet* (2000), insisted that while altruism was a fundamental principle in organ donation it is the recipient's need and not the donor's preference that ought to determine the nature of the exchange. But although the ruling and editorial are clear, they do not really unravel the deeper problems this case raises about the nature of gift giving and the motivations of givers (Scott 2006). What is difficult is that, although we may want to condemn the racism here, we also tend to think that, when it comes to altruism, people should have a say in to whom and how far their beneficence extends and how generous it should be. Arriving at a morally cleansed altruism is not so easy.

Most of us believe that we ought to be able to exercise choice and discretion in our charitable giving. It may not be wrong to prefer the not so needy over the very needy, at least if one does not have a moral obligation to the latter. Our choice of recipients may stem, as we have seen, from a sense of community or solidarity. That may be dismissed as mere sentiment or emotion in contrast to what is morally correct, but in some cases at least solidarity may itself have moral value. Jean Hampton has argued

that when people make choices that foster a close social relationship, they are 'so unified with those whom their acts are
attempting to benefit that what they regard as good for themselves
is what will be good for those with whom they are united'
(Hampton 1993: 158). That may have been true in the organ
donor case, even if the sense of white solidarity the family were
attempting to promote, is racially discriminatory. We need an
answer, then, to the question of when group-bounded altruistic
giving is morally praiseworthy, as with Titmuss's good citizen
blood donors, and when morally condemnable, as in this case.

One answer would be to endorse a rights-based, impartialist
political philosophy which rejects any public role for altruism or
community (De Wispelaere 2004). The latter involves sentiment
and contingency, while only rights mark out the territory of what
we owe to other persons. Such a view, although popular among
liberals and cosmopolitans, has difficulty in explaining the scope
of our responsibilities. Does each person in the world have duties
to every other, and if not how are duties to be distributed? We
shall not address that question here. Instead, we shall explore the
ethics of altruism, and in particular the question of motivation:
what makes us do what we do. As we anticipated in Chapter 2,
there are two strands of thought in the history of altruism (indeed
the history of morality) on the question of motivation. One
prioritizes reason, the other emotion. In contrast to the rights-
based critique which assumes altruism is based on sentiment, we
want to endorse a hybrid view where both reason and emotion are
important in explaining people's altruistic activity. Having done
so, we shall be in a better position to see what is distinctive and
important about the altruistic perspective.

The best case for thinking that altruism is based on reasons, can
be found in Kant's working out of our universal duty of beneficence. As we saw in Chapter 2, Kant sought to understand the
moral rationale behind the Golden Rule – do unto others as they
do unto you. If one was in need it would be irrational, Kant
thought, to forgo receiving assistance from others. If matters were
reversed and we encounter another person who needs our help,
then we ought to be committed to giving assistance. To deny this
would involve an inconsistency in asking for help ourselves but
not being prepared to give it to others. Hence we have a duty to
help others, to be beneficent. Our acknowledgment of that duty
involves our recognition of humanity as needy creatures, and our

own and other's membership of a common humanity. If altruism is interpreted as a form of beneficence then this argument gives us each a good moral reason to be altruistic. Along similar lines, Thomas Nagel argued that altruistic reasons, where one takes the other person's standpoint as important in itself and not just for one's own purposes, are fundamental to morality (Nagel 1970). This complements Bernard Williams' assertion that altruism is fundamental to any morality (Williams 1972: 250), although Williams does not favour the Kantian-based approach, rather a Humean one.

As we saw, Lawrence Blum (1980) provides us with an alternative account which has altruistic emotions at its centre. He too complements the Scottish philosopher, David Hume, whose sentiment-based account of morality we encountered in Chapter 1. Blum argues that our immediate response to another person's need is an emotional one. Even if that response can be rationally evaluated and assessed later on, it is not what motivates us to aid or assist another in the first instance. This seems closer to our every day moral experience than Kant's more rationalistic one in that it takes proper account of the moral tug that pulls us into situations that demand action. Indeed, engaging in abstract thinking may not be appropriate when the demands of another are immediate, and Blum's account restores emotion as a complement to our reason.

Interestingly, the emotion-based perspective on altruism fits neatly with the evolutionary account of its origins since, for the latter, feeling and sentiments are simply psychological mechanisms which cause organisms to behave in adaptively successful ways. If a human or other animal feels pulled towards exhibiting altruism towards its kin, that is just because altruism is a more evolutionarily successful strategy than egotism. The capacity to respond to the needs of others, however sophisticated the role it now has in human socialisation, is simply one more ability that helps perpetuate the species, alongside the capacity for recognition and memory, and the capacity to anticipate the future. The problem with including emotionally motivated altruism within evolutionary biology, however, is that, as we have seen, the latter evacuates altruism of its distinctively moral content. It explains why altruistic behaviour is caused in humans, but it cannot supply reasons to be altruistic. But in contrast to insects, among other simple organisms, human beings deliberate on their reasons for being altruistic. We are moral agents who reflect on our altruism and are not simply pulled towards it by psychological forces manifesting themselves as emotions. To put morality back into altruism, we need to be able to show how we act not merely to achieve certain desires, where reason has a purely instrumental role, but how reason itself sets our goals and motivates us to pursue them. Blum's and other sense-based accounts of altruism are not capable of taking us that far. Neither is Sober and Wilson's attempt at arguing in favour of motivational pluralism, although they do admit that their position is descriptive, seeking simply to explain modes of human behaviour. Kant's argument for the duty of beneficence, by contrast, is an example of reason dictating why altruistic goals are worth pursuing. The motivation to be altruistic can be supported by both belief states about what one ought to do and also desires.

Sober and Wilson's motivational pluralism is not to be confused with moral pluralism. They rejected the view that there are either altruists *or* egoists; rather they believe that a range of motivations come into play when confronted by the demands of action. Whether or not we are moral pluralists is a different question. To find out how reason does function to motivate us draws us into an ongoing philosophical debate between motivational internalism and motivational externalism. The latter holds that the relationship between motivation and moral judgement is contingent, the former that a necessary connection exists between moral judgement and motivation to act on that judgement (Rosati 1996). It would be a considerable challenge for further research to discover whether internalism or externalism lines up best with an evolutionary approach to altruism, picking up where Sober and Wilson's motivational pluralism has left off. Kant's theory argues for motivational internalism. Once I have established reasons for being beneficent or altruistic, to not act on those reasons, that is, to not recognize their motivational force may well be possible, but only on pain of extreme irrationality. Motivational externalism makes no such strong link.

We have in this book surveyed altruism's meaning, history and limits, and its use by sociobiologists, psychologists and economists, among others. We hope we have demonstrated its importance in the social sciences and philosophy. But why should altruism continue to be an important idea in human thought? Is it perhaps a concept whose career is largely over, relevant at a certain historical epoch, but no longer? One reason for maintaining altruism's relevance, we maintain, is that it marks out a distinct position in moral philosophy. Some ethicists equate altruism with moral philosophy itself and, as we saw in Chapter 4, almost all psychologists do so. But altruism does not encompass the moral point of view *per se*; the latter is too rich and multi-faceted to be capturable by a single concept and, as we've seen, altruism while closely related to some moral concepts (such as benevolence or sympathy) finds it hard to accommodate others (such as impartiality or rights). We commonly think of altruism as something one enacts. The altruist is the do-gooder; the person who gives to Oxfam, shovels snow from their neighbour's front yard or rescues the drowning child. This is not incorrect, but as we have stressed in this book it is the motivation which powers the action, and the possible sacrifice that it entails, that is important for altruism. Altruism, then, is also a *perspective* and what distinguishes the altruistic perspective from the perspective of morality *per se* is well captured by Monroe's notion of a common humanity. As we saw in Chapter 4, the idea of a common humanity conjures up a vision of a world where individuals are all members of the human family, the bonds that exist between them being inestimably more important than surface differences of race or creed. A person with this perspective sees the human in every person they encounter (just as the rescuers of Jews in the Second World War saw Jews not as sub-human or as especially worthy, but simply as needy human beings). The notion of a common humanity has more substance to it than the idea that all human beings are equal. The latter is of course a core moral idea, and is at the heart of doctrines of rights and impartiality. But a common humanity goes beyond the bare notion of each person being an equal in urging us to attend to the spark of the human in each person, their needs, vulnerabilities and predicament at the specific time we encounter them, and it urges us to form a relation to them unmediated by prior social roles. An example can be found at the beginning of Michael Ignatieff's book, *The Needs of Strangers*:

> I live in a market street in north London. Every Tuesday morning there is a barrow outside my door and a cluster of old age pensioners rummage through torn curtains, button-less shirts, stained vests, frayed trousers and faded dresses

that the barrow man has to offer ... I imagine them living
alone in small dark rooms lit by the glow of electric
heaters. I came upon an old man once doing his shopping
alone, weighed down in a queue at a potato stall and nearly
fainting from tiredness. I made him sit down in a pub
while I did the rest of his shopping.

(Ignatieff 2001: 9)

One might ask, did Ignatieff have a duty to help the old man?
Common sense morality would say that he did not or, as the more
technical language of moral philosophy has it, that his duty was
merely a supererogatory one. Again this is not incorrect, but it is
not the whole story. For in helping the old man Ignatieff (we may
suppose) saw him in a different way than the others who did not
help. He related to him in that moment as a fellow human being
with needs and vulnerabilities. In transcending our given roles,
altruism is often creative behaviour. All of us assist each other in
myriads of ways all the time, but it is not altruistic for the
librarian to give you the library book or the driver to stop for you
at a red traffic light. In thinking in terms of a common humanity,
we very often transcend our established institutional roles and
moral requirements since these requirements typically pick out
only part of humanity as relevant to our actions. We form a
connection with another person in our minds and make that
connection real by thinking of what, here and now, we can do to
help them. Sometimes this is obvious (saving the drowning
child), often it is not (setting up a charity to help street children).
Either way, in acting altruistically, we show ourselves to be, at
least for that moment, extrinsic persons connected to our fellow
human beings through bonds stronger than those uniting any
particular group.

Still, we may ask, do we need the perspective on morality that
altruism gives us? The reasons for scepticism stem from scepticism about altruism. If people's needs are important, one can
argue, then the care they require should be institutionally provided. If their needs are not important then there is no special
virtue in showing them altruism. So, we might question, more
practically what has happened to the welfare system that it leaves
children on the street at night or vulnerable old people to their
own resources? It is our moral failure, so this argument goes, that
such avenues for altruism are present in our society. But this reply

is unconvincing for two reasons. To begin with, there is plenty of help we can and do give to other people which is important, if not vital, and which has significant positive social consequences. We should not say it is not altruistic to offer a friend a lift home just because they are perfectly capable of taking public transport. Indeed, these kind of everyday altruistic acts serve to cement our friendship.

To take another example, it is altruistic, indeed creatively altruistic, for me to donate the prize for the tombola at my local infants school's summer fair and, again, while this has positive consequences for the community it is not required nor is it altruism of the first order. But there is also a deeper reason for resisting the view that altruism is either institutionalizable or not really altruism and for retaining the perspective on morality that it offers us. The reason is that we want there to be a space beyond obligation, beyond strict justice, where we can demonstrate our goodness to others in ways that manifest the common humanity we share with them. Consider the person who devotes three years of their life to doing VSO (Voluntary Service Overseas) work in Africa. No theory of morality would require them to do so, but they are doing palpable, indeed crucial, good. But we miss the point if we say that their action is praiseworthy but supererogatory and leave it at that. We want to know why it is praiseworthy. In leaving the comforts of their home, in seeking to understand the needs and points of view of strangers far away, and in forging connections with them, the VSO worker exhibits creative altruism and adds value to the world. Unless they have some special prior connection to Africa, it looks like they are motivated by the idea of a common humanity. In cultivating the idea of a common humanity, and in maintaining institutions, such as VSO, where it can flourish (something we can all play a part in), we enact altruism in the world.

Here is another example. Many countries have institutions, such as Local Exchange Trading Systems (LETS) or timebanks, where individuals can offer their skills to others and in return receive the benefits of others' skilled labour without any money changing hands. In many local communities there is a non-monetary economy of babysitting, gardening, yoga lessons and car maintenance. It might seem that, because the notion of exchange remains central here (one hour's car maintenance is worth two hour's work in the garden, and so on), LETS, timebanks and the like, are not venues for altruism at all. But it depends very much on the participants' motives for trading their labour. Few shopkeepers are greatly concerned for your welfare when they sell you a good. But non-market economies enable participants to identify others with particular needs and to exercise a degree of creative altruism in offering to meet them with skills of their own. The labour they receive in return may or may not, in their eyes, be worth as much as the labour they offer (unlike in a market where sellers are rarely willing to make a loss).

This is quite different from welfare states which are impersonal and financed through compulsory taxation. It is true that altruism need not be present in these sorts of schemes, but that is often true with altruistic acts. We would normally think a person who gives thousands to charity an altruistic individual, but if they publicise their giving among influential people we may begin to question their motives. LETS and timebanks are, therefore, like VSO, another institutional venue for altruism – and a counterpoint to the argument sometimes made that altruism cannot be institutionalized. As we suggested above, it is unduly stipulative to insist that altruism must involve sacrifice, and it is reasonable for those who help others for others' sake nonetheless to want something in return. In a similar but less dramatic way than VSO, reciprocal institutions, such as LETS, also provide channels for goodness and encourage their members to see others as part of a common humanity. It is a small, but important, piece of altruism to offer babysitting to a single mother in return for her feeding your pets, but if she is a stranger and you don't have children yourself, the idea of a common humanity has a modest role.

How then might we encourage altruism and the attitudes and virtues that accompany it? The question is not an easy one, especially in societies such as our own where individuals are keen to assert their rights and often willing to meet only those duties that are strictly required by law (and sometimes not even those). Since altruism is dependent so crucially on motivation it is not something which is easily fostered. The solution is to employ an indirect approach, and here two complementary strategies might be identified. The first is to create new institutions in which altruism can flower and be publicly demonstrated. We have discussed some altruistic institutions. Other examples might include schemes for volunteers to help children with their reading at school, measures to make it easier for employees to donate a fraction of their salary to good causes (this is already quite common in the United States) and encouraging working citizens to give a few hours a month volunteering for a charitable organization (some people have particular skills to offer, such as law or IT). If flexible working were more commonplace, or even better paid or career breaks were introduced, it would be easier for working people to find the time to help others in these sorts of ways.

A further altruism-friendly institutional reform would be the introduction of a citizens' or basic income: an unconditional benefit paid to every adult citizen which would replace the vast panoply of existing welfare benefits. A basic income scheme would enable people to take time off work or work part-time while simultaneously engaging in unpaid altruistic work. Sometimes it is a case not so much of creating a new location for altruistic endeavour but rather giving institutional recognition to forms of altruism already practised. Consider, for example, the very large numbers of people who are carers of infirm parents, children or spouses, in many states these form a substantial but often invisible proportion of the population. Caring is by its nature a fairly isolating experience. But recognizing care work, through, for example, employing more paid professionals to assist carers and to enable them to take time off, and providing clubs and associations for them to meet is a good way of helping maintain this vital form of altruism. These strategies, however, are of little use unless people are motivated to engage in altruistic activity in the first place. For that reasom it is important that altruism is seen to be done: it can be infectious.

The other strategy is social and political reforms which make it more likely that people will want to help others. The Oliners, for example, urge a more direct strategy and argue for more teaching of altruism and the virtues of pro-social behaviour in schools, as valuable in themselves and an antidote to the instrumental skills of literacy and numeracy (Oliner and Oliner 1988). Children might be taught about altruistic exemplars, such as Carnegie heroes in the US and gentile rescuers of Jews in wartime Europe. The firefighters and police officers who risked their lives to rescue survivors from the 9/11 attack on the World Trade Center is a more contemporary example. The Oliners' strategy might be a little optimistic for it is not clear how much influence altruistic stories will have on children once they graduate from school. But as part of a wider curriculum that emphasizes our duties to others, the idea may have some merit. Other suggestions have been a little more oblique.

Piliavin and her colleagues conjecture that more mixing of different social classes and ethnic groups would help build bridges between individuals with otherwise very different life experiences, and thus help in a small way to foster an ethic of common humanity. (Encouraging self-attribution of responsibility and a faith in one's own competence are other strategies (Piliavin *et. al.* 1981: ch.10).) The view that inclusion fosters altruism needs to take account of the fact there is much *intra*-group altruism too. New immigrants who arrive in a strange city often head straight for the community of expatriots from whence they came to get help in housing and finding work. Perhaps we might better say that social mixing might help motivate altruism, of a liberal kind, that is *inter*-group altruism. If so, then public policy on planning regulations, the design of public housing and local democracy, could have a positive role in promoting contact and thus, we might hope, altruistic practices, between members of different sorts of social groups.

As a general rule, the more indirect strategy, which tries to create the sorts of social conditions in which people will come to have more altruistic motives by themselves, may be a better one to pursue than the more direct one, where the state simply extols the virtues of a more altruistic lifestyle. The latter has a whiff of paternalism about it, however well intentioned. Closing the income and wealth gap between rich and poor, and other measures to combat social exclusion, may also have altruism-friendly effects, as citizens come to regard themselves more as partners in a common social enterprise. But as with almost all suggestions for fostering a more altruistic society, in order to know how effective policies are, we would need to conduct some social scientific research.

Bibliography

Anheier, H. K. and Lent, D. (2006) *Creative Philanthropy.* London: Routledge.

Archard, D. (2002) Selling yourself: Titmuss's arguments against a market in blood, *Journal of Ethics*, 6: 87–103.

Aristotle (1976) *Nicomachean Ethics*, trans. J. A. K. Thompson. London: Penguin Books.

Aristotle (1981) *Eudemian Ethics*, trans. H. Rackman. Cambridge, MA: Harvard University Press.

Arneson, R. (1997) Egalitarianism and the Undeserving Poor, *Journal of Political Philosophy* 5(3): 327–50. Available at http://philosophyfaculty.ucsd.edu/faculty/rarneson/undeser3.pdf (accessed 11 May 2007).

Arrow, K. (1972) Gifts and exchanges, *Philosophy and Public Affairs,* 1(4): 343–62.

Aquinas, T. (1964) *Summa Theologica.* London: Blackfriars, Eyre and Spottiswood.

Axelrod, R. (1984) *The Evolution of Cooperation.* New York, NY: Basic Books.

Axelrod, R. (1986) An evolutionary approach to norms, *American Political Science Review*, 80: 1101–11.

Baron, M. (1987) Kantian ethics and supererogation, *The Journal of Philosophy*, 84: 237–62.

Baron, M. (1997) Kantian ethics and the claims of detachment, in R. M. Schott (ed.) *Feminist Interpretations of Immanuel Kant.* Pennsylvania, PA: Pennsylvania State University Press.

Barry, B. (1995) *Justice as Impartiality.* Oxford: Oxford University Press.

Batson, C. D. (1991) *The Altruism Question: Towards a Social-Psychological Answer.* Hillsdale, NJ: Lawrence Erlbaum.

Batson, C. D. (2002) Addressing the altruism question experimentally, in S. G. Post (ed.) *Altruism and Altruistic Love*. Oxford: Oxford University Press.

Becker, G. (1981) *A Treatise on the Family*. Cambridge, MA: Harvard University Press.

Blum, L. (1980) *Friendship, Altruism and Morality*. London: Routledge & Kegan Paul.

Blum, L. (1992) Altruism and the moral value of rescue: resisting persecution, racism and genocide, in P. M. Oliner *et al*. (eds) *Embracing the Other: Philosophical, Psychological and Historical Perspectives on Altruism*. New York, NY: New York University Press.

Boehm, C. (2000) Conflict and the evolution of social control, *Journal of Consciousness Studies*, 7(1–2): 79–101.

Bowlin, J. (1999) *Contingency and Fortune in Aquinas' Ethics*. Cambridge: Cambridge University Press.

Brody, B. (1987) The role of private philanthropy, in E. F. Paul, *et al*. (eds) *Beneficence, Philanthropy and the Public Good*. Oxford: Basil Blackwell.

Brosnahan,T. (1907) *The Catholic Encyclopaedia*. Available at: www.newadvent.org.cathen/01369a.htm (accessed 14 November 2003).

Buchanan, A. (1996) Charity, justice and the idea of progress, in J. B. Schneewind (ed.) *Giving*. Bloomington, IN: Indiana University Press.

Churchill, R. P. and Street, E. (2004) Is there a paradox of altruism? in J. Seglow (ed.) *The Ethics of Altruism*. London: Frank Cass.

Collard, D. (1978) *Altruism and the Economy: A Study in Non-Selfish Economics*. Oxford: Martin Robertson.

Collins, F. H. (1895) *The Epitome of Synthetic Philosophy of Herbert Spencer*. New York, NY: Appleton & Co.

Comte, A. ([1851] 1969–70) *Système de politique positive*: *Oeuvres d'Auguste Comte Tomes 7–10*. Paris: Editions Anthropos.

Comte, A. ([1852] 1966) *Cathechisme Positive*. Paris: Garniers-Flammarions.

Cumberland, R. (1672) *A Treatise of the Laws of Nature*. Available at: http://olldownload.libertyfund.org/EBooks/ Cumberland_0996.pdf (accessed 23 February 2007).

Darley, J. M. and Batson, C. D. (1973) 'From Jerusalem to Jericho': A study of situational and dispositional variables in helping behaviour, *Journal of Personality and Social Psychology,* 27(1): 100–8.

Darwin, C. (1871) *The Descent of Man,* 1st edn. London: John Murray.

Darwin, C. (1874) *The Descent of Man,* 2nd edn. Chicago, IL: Rand, McNally & Co.

Davis, J. (1992) *Exchange.* Buckingham: Open University Press.

Dawkins, R. (1976) *The Selfish Gene.* Oxford: Oxford University Press.

de Waal, F. B. M. (1996) *Good Natured: The Origins of Right and Wrong in Humans and Other Animals.* Cambridge, MA: Harvard University Press.

De Wispelaere, J. (2004) Altruism, impartiality and moral demands, in J. Seglow (ed.) *The Ethics of Altruism.* London: Frank Cass.

den Uyl, D. J. (1987) The right to welfare and the virtue of charity, in E. F. Paul *et al.* (eds) *Beneficence, Philanthropy and the Public Good.* Oxford: Basil Blackwell.

Dennett, D. (1995) *Darwin's Dangerous Idea.* London: Penguin Books.

Douglas, M. (2002) Foreword, in M. Mauss, *The Gift.* London: Routledge.

Dryzek, J. and Goodin, R. E. (1986) Risk-sharing and social justice: the motivational foundations of the post-war welfare state, *British Journal of Political Science,* 16(1): 1–34.

Dugatkin, L.A. (2002) Co-operation in animals: an evolutionary overview, *Biology and Philosophy,* 17(4): 459–76.

Durkheim, E. ([1897] 1970) G. Simpson (ed.) *Suicide.* London: Routledge & Kegan Paul.

Dworkin, R. (1977) *Taking Rights Seriously.* Cambridge MA: Harvard University Press.

Fabre, C. (2004) Good Samaritanism: a matter of justice, in J. Seglow (ed.) *The Ethics of Altruism.* London: Frank Cass.

Fehr, E. and Fischerbacher, U. (2005) Altruists with green beards, *Analyse und Kritik,* 27(1): 73–84.

Ferguson, J. E. (1993) *Giving More Than a Damn: A Study of Household and Individual Charitable Contributions.* New York, NY: Garland.

Frank, R. H. (2005) Altruists with green beards: still kicking? *Analyse und Kritik* 27(1): 85–96.

Gewirth, A. (1978) *Reason and Morality*. Chicago, IL: University of Chicago Press.

Gewirth, A. (1987) Private philanthropy and positive rights, in E. F. Paul *et al*. (eds) *Beneficence, Philanthropy and the Public Good*. Oxford: Basil Blackwell.

Gilligan, C. (1982) *In a Different Voice: Psychological Theory and Women's Development*. Cambridge, MA: Harvard University Press.

Godelier, M. (1999) *The Enigma of the Gift*. Cambridge: Polity.

Goodin, R. E. (1988) *Reasons for Welfare*. Princeton: Princeton University Press.

Gould, S. J. (1980) Sociobiology and the theory of natural selection, in M. Ruse (ed.) *The Philosophy of Biology*. London: Macmillan.

Hamilton, W. D. (1964) The genetic evolution of social behaviour I – II, *Journal of Theoretical Biology*, 7: 1–52.

Hampton, J. (1993) Selflessness and loss of self, *Social Philosophy and Policy*, 10(1): 135–65.

Hansson, R. O. and Slade, K. M. (1977) Altruism toward a deviant in city and small town, *Journal of Applied Social Psychology*, 7(3): 272–9.

Harris, D. (1987) *Justifying State Welfare*. Oxford: Basil Blackwell.

Harris, J. (2003). Gifting organs is no different from their sale, *The Guardian*, 5 December.

Herman, B. (1993) *The Practice of Moral Judgement*. Cambridge MA: Harvard University Press.

Hobbes, T. ([1651] 1996), R. Tuck (ed.) *Leviathan*. Cambridge: Cambridge University Press.

Holy Bible, New International Version, International Bible Society.

Hume, D. ([1739–40] 1888) in L. A. Selby-Bigge (ed.) *A Treatise on Human Nature*. Oxford: Clarendon Press.

Hume, D. ([1777] 1975) *Inquiries Concerning Human Understanding and Concerning the Principles of Morals*. Oxford: Oxford University Press.

Huxley, T. H. (1898) Evolution and ethics, in *Evolution and Ethics and Other Essays*. New York, NY: D. Appleton.

IEA (Institute of Economic Affairs) (1968) *The Price of Blood*. London: IEA.

Ignatieff, M. (2001) *The Needs of Strangers*. London: Picador.

Jansen, V. A. A. and van Baalen, M. (2006) Altruism through beard chromodynamics, *Nature* (30 March), 440: 663–6.

Jollimore, T. (2006) Impartiality, *The Stanford Encyclopedia of Philosophy*. Avalable at: http://plato.stanford.edu/entries/impartiality/ (accessed 23 February 2007).

Jordan, B. (1989) *The Common Good*. Oxford: Basil Blackwell.

Jordan, M. D. (1993) Theology and philosophy, in N. Kretzman and E. Stump (eds) *The Cambridge Companion to Aquinas*. Cambridge: Cambridge University Press.

Kant, I. ([1785] 1996) Groundwork to the metaphysics of morals, in M. J. Gregor (trans. and ed.) *Practical Philosophy*, Cambridge edition of the works of Immanuel Kant. Cambridge: Cambridge University Press.

Kant, I. ([1797] 1996) Metaphysics of morals, in M. J. Gregor (trans. and ed.) *Practical Philosophy* Cambridge edition of the works of Immanuel Kant. Cambridge: Cambridge University Press.

Karylowski, J. (1984) Focus of attention and altruism: endocentric and exocentric sources of altruistic behaviour, in E. Staub *et al.* (eds) *Development and Maintenance of Pro-Social Behaviour*. New York, NY: Plenum Press.

Katz, L. (2000) Towards good and evil: evolutionary approaches to aspects of human morality, in L. Katz (ed.) *Evolutionary Origins of Morality*. Bowling Green, KY: Imprint Academic.

Kitcher, P. (1993) The evolution of human altruism, *Journal of Philosophy*, 90(10): 497–516.

Kohlberg, L. (1981) *The Philosophy of Moral Development: Moral Stages and the Idea of Justice*, Essays on Moral Development Vol 1. San Francisco, CA: Harper & Row.

Kohn, A. (1990) *The Brighter Side of Human Nature: Altruism and Empathy in Everyday Life*. New York, NY: Basic Books.

Kolm, S. C. (2000a) Introduction: the economics of reciprocity, giving and altruism, in L. - A. Gérard-Varet *et al.* (eds) *The Economics of Reciprocity, Giving and Altruism*. Basingstoke: Macmillan.

Kolm, S. C. (2000b) The theory of reciprocity, in L. - A. Gérard-Varet, *et al.* (eds) *The Economics of Reciprocity, Giving and Altruism*. Basingstoke: Macmillan.

Konarzewski, K. (1992) Empathy and protest: two roots of heroic altruism, in P. Oliner *et al.* (eds) *Embracing the Other: Philosophical, Psychological and Historical Perspectives on Altruism.* New York, NY: New York University Press.

Korsgaard, C. (1996) *Creating the Kingdom of Ends.* New York NY: Cambridge University Press.

Krebs, D. L. (1970) Altruism: an examination of the concept and a review of the literature, *Psychological Bulletin,* 73: 258–302.

Krebs, D. L. (1982) Psychological approaches to altruism, *Ethics,* 92(3): 447–58.

Krebs, D. L. and van Hesteren, F. (1992) The development of altruistic personality, in P. Oliner *et al.* (eds) *Embracing the Other: Philosophical, Psychological and Historical Perspectives on Altruism.* New York, NY: New York University Press.

Krebs, D. L. and van Hesteren, F. (1994) The development of altruism: toward an integrative model, *Developmental Review,* 14: 1–56.

Kropotkin, P. ([1910] 1987) *Mutual Aid: A Factor in Evolution,* in J. Hewetson (ed.) London: Freedom Press.

Latané, B. and Darley, J. M. (1970) *The Unresponsive Bystander: Why Doesn't He Help?* New York, NY: Appleton-Century-Crofts.

Lawler, J. (1999) The moral world of the Simpson family, in W. Irwin *et al.* (eds) *The Simpsons and Philosophy: The D'oh of Homer.* Peru, IL: Carus Publishing Company.

Le Grand, J. (1997) Afterword, in R. Titmuss, *The Gift Relationship.* New York, NY: The New Press.

Lightman, E. S. (1981) Continuity in social behaviours: the case of voluntary blood donation, *Journal of Social Policy,* 10(2): 53–79.

Lomasky, L. (1983), Gift relations, sexual relations and freedom, *Philosophical Quarterly,* 33(132): 250–8.

Losco, J. (1986) Understanding altruism: a comparison of various models, *Political Psychology,* 7(2): 323–48.

Lunati, M. T. (1997) *Ethical Issues in Economics: From Altruism to Co-operation to Equity.* Basingstoke: Palgrave.

Machan, T. (1997) Blocked exchanges revisited, *Journal of Applied Philosophy,* 14(3): 249–62.

Malinowski, B. (1932) *Argonauts of the Western Pacific.* London: Routledge & Kegan Paul.

Mansbridge, J. (1990) Expanding the range of formal modelling, in J. Mansbridge (ed.) *Beyond Self-Interest.* Chicago, IL: University of Chicago Press.

Maris, C. W. (1981) *Critique of the Empiricist Explanation of Morality.* Deventer: Kluwer.

Mauss, M. ([1950] 2002) M. Douglas (ed.) *The Gift.* London: Routledge.

Maynard Smith, J. (1988) *Games, Sex and Evolution.* London: Harvester Books.

Midlarsky, E. (1992) Helping in late life, in P. Oliner *et al.* (eds) *Embracing the Other: Philosophical, Psychological and Historical Perspectives on Altruism.* New York, NY: New York University Press.

Milgram, S. (1970) The experience of living in cities, *Science,* 167: 1461–8.

Miller, D. (1989) *Market, State and Community.* Oxford: Oxford University Press.

Miller, D. (2004) 'Are they *my* poor?': the problem of altuism in a world of strangers, in J. Seglow (ed.) *The Ethics of Altruism.* London: Frank Cass.

Monroe, K. R. (1994) A fat lady in a corset: altruism and social theory, *American Journal of Political Science,* 38(4): 861–93.

Monroe, K. R. (1996) *The Heart of Altruism: Perceptions of a Common Humanity.* Princeton, NJ: Princeton University Press.

Monroe, K. R. (2002) Explicating altruism, in S. G. Post (ed.) *Altruism and Altruistic Love.* Oxford: Oxford University Press.

Monroe, K. R. *et al.* (1990) Altruism and the theory of rational action: rescuers of Jews in Nazi Europe, *Ethics,* 101(1): 103–22;

Nadler, A. and Fisher, J. D. (1984) Effects of donor–recipient relationships on recipients reactions to aid, in E. Staub *et al.* (eds) *Development and Maintenance of Pro-Social Behaviour.* New York, NY: Plenum Press.

Nagel, T. (1970) *The Possibility of Altruism.* Princeton, NJ: Princeton University Press.

Nagel, T. (1991) *Equality and Partiality.* Oxford: Oxford University Press.

Nietzsche, F. ([1881] 1982) *Daybreak,* trans. R. J. Hollingdale. Cambridge: Cambridge University Press.

Nietzsche, F. ([1901] 1968) *The Will To Power*. trans. W. Kaufmann and R. J. Hollingdale. New York, NY: Vintage Books.

Nietzsche, F. ([1910] 1992) *On the Genealogy of Morals* in *The Basic Writings of Nietzsche*, trans. W. Kaufmann. New York, NY: The Modern Library.

O'Connor, J. (1987) Philanthropy and selfishness, in E. F. Paul *et al.* (eds) *Beneficence, Philanthropy and the Public Good*. Oxford: Basil Blackwell.

O'Hear, A. (1997) *Beyond Evolution*. Oxford: Clarendon Press.

Oldenquist, A. (1990) The origins of morality: an essay in philosophical anthropology, *Social Philosophy and Policy,* 8(1): 121–40.

Oliner, S. P. and Oliner, P. M. (1988) *The Altruistic Personality: Rescuers of Jews in Nazi Europe*. New York, NY: Free Press.

Page, R. M. (1996) *Altruism and the British Welfare State*. Aldershot: Avebury.

Parfit, D. (1983) *Reasons and Persons*. Oxford: Oxford University Press.

Phelps, E. S. (1975) Introduction, in E. S. Phelps (ed.) *Altruism, Morality and Economic Theory*. New York, NY: Russell Sage Foundation.

Piliavin, J. A. *et al.* (1969) Good Samaritanism: an underground phenomenon? *Journal of Personality and Social Psychology,* 13: 289–99.

Piliavin, J. A. *et al.* (1981) *Emergency Intervention*. New York, NY: Academic Press.

Prochaska, F. K. (1988) *The Voluntary Impulse*. London: Faber & Faber.

Pufendorf, S. ([1673] 1991) *On the Duty of Man and Citizen According to Natural Law*, J. Tully ed. and M. Silverthorne (trans.). Cambridge: Cambridge University Press.

Radcliffe-Richards, J. (2000) *Human Nature after Darwin*. London: Routledge.

Ridley, M. (1997) *The Origins of Virtue*. Harmondsworth: Penguin Books.

Rosati, C. (1996) Internalism and the good for a person, *Ethics,* 106: 297–326.

Rosen, S. (1984) Some paradoxical implications of helping and being helped, in E. Staub *et al.* (eds) *Development and Maintenance of Pro-Social Behaviour*. New York, NY: Plenum Press.

Rosenberg, A. (1998) Altruism: theoretical contexts, in D. Hull and M. Ruse (eds) *The Philosophy of Biology*. Oxford: Oxford University Press.

Rosenhan, D. (1970) The natural socialization of altruistic autonomy, in J. Macaulay and L. Berkowitz (eds) *Altruism And Helping Behaviour: Social Psychological Studies Of Some Antecedents And Consequences*. New York, NY: Academic Press.

Ruse, M. (1973) *The Philosophy of Biology*. London: Hutchinson and Co.

Ruse, M. (1990) Evolutionary ethics and the search for predecessors: Kant, Hume and all the way back to Aristotle? *Social Philosophy and Policy*, 8(1): 59–85.

Ruse, M. (1991) The significance of evolution, in P. Singer (ed.) *A Companion to Ethics*. Oxford: Blackwell.

Rushton, J. P. (1980) *Altruism, Socialization and Society*. Englewood Cliffs, NJ: Prentice-Hall Inc.

Rushton, J. P. (1982) Altruism in society: a social learning perspective, *Ethics*, 92: 425–46.

Ryan, A. (1996) The philanthropic perspective after a hundred years, in J. B. Schneewind (ed.) *Giving*. Bloomington, IN: Indiana University Press.

Sahlins, M. ([1972] 2004) *Stone Age Economics*. London: Routledge.

Salter, F. S. (ed.) (2004) *Welfare, Ethnicity and Altruism: New Findings and Evolutionary Theory*. London: Frank Cass.

Scheler, M. (1954) Werke, *Historisches Wortebuch der Philosophie*. Basel: Schwabe & Co.

Schneewind, J. B. (1996) Philosophical ideas of charity: some historical reflections, in J. B. Schneewind (ed.) *Giving*. Bloomington, IN: Indiana University Press.

Schokkaert, E. and van Ootegem, L. (2000) Preference variation and private donations, in L. - A. Gérard-Varet *et al.* (eds) *The Economics of Reciprocity, Giving and Altruism*. Basingstoke: Macmillan.

Schroeder, W. (2000) Continental ethics, in H. LaFollette (ed.) *The Blackwell Guide to Ethical Theory*. Oxford: Blackwell.

Scott, N. (2004) Is altruism a moral duty? *Imprints: A Journal of Analytical Socialism*, 7(3).

Scott, N. (2006) Conditions, preferences and race in organ donation, *Journal of International Biotechnology Law*, 3(2): 57–62.

Seglow, J. (2004) Altruism and freedom, in J. Seglow (ed.) *The Ethics of Altruism*. London: Frank Cass.

Sen, A. (1977) Rational fools: a critique of the behavioural foundations of economic theory, *Philosophy and Public Affairs*, 6(4): 317–44.

Shaftesbury, Earl of ([1711] 1977) *Inquiry Concerning Virtue and Merit*, D. Walford (ed.). Manchester: Manchester University Press.

Singer, P. (1972) Famine, affluence and morality, *Philosophy and Public Affairs*, 1(1): 229–43.

Singer, P. (1973) Altruism and commerce: a defense of Titmuss against Arrow, *Philosophy and Public Affairs*, 2(3): 312–20.

Singer, P. (1977) Freedoms and utilities in the distribution of health care, in G. Dworkin *et al.* (eds) *Markets and Morals*. Washington, DC: Hemisphere Publishing Corporation.

Smith, A. ([1776] 1976) *An Enquiry into the Nature and Causes of the Wealth of Nations*, R. H. Campbell and A. S. Skinner (eds). Oxford: Clarendon Press.

Smith, A. ([1790] 2002) *The Theory of Moral Sentiments*, Knud Haakonssen (ed.) Cambridge: Cambridge University Press.

Sober, E. (1998) What is evolutionary altruism? in D. Hull and M. Ruse (eds) *The Philosophy of Biology*. Oxford: Oxford University Press.

Sober, E. and Wilson, D. S. (1998) *Unto Others: The Evolution and Psychology of Unselfish Behaviour*. Cambridge, MA: Harvard University Press.

Sober, E. and Wilson, D. S. (2000) Summary of unto others, in L. Katz (ed.), *Evolutionary Origins of Morality: Cross Disciplinary Perspectives*. Bowling Green: Imprint Academic.

Spencer, H. (1872) *The Principles of Psychology*. London: Williams and Norgate.

Spencer, H. (1879) *The Data of Ethics*. London: Williams and Norgate.

Spencer, H. (1892) *Principles of Ethics*. London: Williams and Norgate.

Stark, O. (1995) *Altruism and Beyond*. Cambridge: Cambridge University Press.

Staub, E. (1978) *Positive Social Behaviour and Morality,* Vol. I Social and Personal Influences. New York, NY: Academic Press.

Thompson, J. L. (1982) Human nature and social explanation, in S. Rose (ed.) *Against Biological Determinism*. New York, NY: Alison and Busby.

Titmuss, R. (1950) *Problems of Social Policy*. London: HMSO and Longman.

Titmuss, R. (1968) *Commitment to Welfare*. London: George Allen & Unwin.

Titmuss, R. ([1970] 1997) *The Gift Relationship*, in A. Oakley and J. Ashton (eds). New York, NY: The New Press.

Trivers, R. L. (1971) The evolution of reciprocal altruism, *Quarterly Review of Biology*, 46: 35–57.

van den Berghe, P. (1981) *The Ethnic Phenomenon*. New York, NY: Elsevier.

Walzer, M. (1992) What does it mean to be an American? *Social Research*, 57.

Ware, A. (1990) Meeting needs through voluntary action: does market society corrode altruism? in A. Ware and R. E. Goodin (eds) *Needs and Welfare*. London: Sage.

Williams, B. (1972) *Morality: An Introduction to Ethics*. Harmondsworth: Penguin.

Wilson, E. O. (1975) *Sociobiology: The New Synthesis*. Cambridge, MA: Harvard University Press.

Wolf, S. (1982) Moral saints, *Journal of Philosophy*, 49(8): 419–39.

Wolff, C. (1720) *Vernünftige Gedanken von der Menschen Thun und Lassen zur Beförderung ihrer Glückseligkeit* [Rational Thoughts on Man's Acts of Commission and Omission, with a View to Advancing His Happiness]. Munich: Halle.

Worchel, S. (1984) The darker side of helping: the social dynamics of helping and co-operation, in E. Staub et al. (eds) *Development and Maintenance of Pro-Social Behaviour*. New York, NY: Plenum Press.

Wynne-Edwards, V. C. (1962) *Animal Dispersion in Relation to Social Behaviour*. Edinburgh: Oliver and Boyd.

Index